The Essential English Grammar

L. G. Alexander

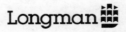

Longman Group UK Limited
Longman House, Burnt Mill, Harlow,
Essex, CM20 2JE England
and Associated Companies throughout the world

Distributed in the United States of America by
Longman Publishing Group, 10 Bank Street, White Plains,
NY 10606 - 1951.

First published 1993

British Library Cataloguing in Publication Data
Alexander, L. G.
Essential English Grammar
I. Title
425

Library of Congress Cataloging-in-Publication Data
Alexander, L. G.
The essential English grammar / L. G. Alexander.
    p.   cm.
Includes index.
ISBN 0-582-21869-1 : £3.50
1. English language—Textbooks for foreign speakers. 2. English
language—Grammar.   I. Title.
PE1128.A4565   1993
428.2'4—dc20   92-33523
                                                    CIP

Set in 9 on 10.8 pt Adobe Helvetica
Produced by Longman Singapore Publishers (Pte) Ltd
Printed in Singapore

ISBN 0 582 21869 1

CONTENTS

INTRODUCTION

Who is this book for and what does it do?
The Essential English Grammar is for students of English at any level who would like to have a handy summary of the key features of English as a foreign or second language. It takes the user right to the heart of English and provides basic information about every important area of study (see Contents page). A summary of the most vital concepts of the English language is included on pages 55-58. This is followed by an Appendix (pages 59-74), which consists of 31 useful sections illustrating key grammatical areas.

How should the book be used?
The book may be used in a variety of ways, for example:

1   It is short enough to be read from cover to cover, so that the reader has an overview and clear summary of the essential facts about English.

2   Particular chapters can be read repeatedly, until the essential features are actively acquired and retained.

3   It can be used as a constant companion and reference work to answer particular questions about English and to provide examples. For more detailed discussion and illustration, consult the *Longman English Grammar*.

The Essential English Grammar has been distilled from the works that have preceded it and which form part of this series:

> *Longman English Grammar* (1988)
> *Longman English Grammar Practice* (1990)
> *Step by Step, Books 1-3* (1991)
> *Longman Advanced Grammar* (1993)

1 Nouns

1.1 What is a noun?

Nouns are the names we give to people, things, places, etc. in order to identify them. For example, a noun can be the name of a person *(John)*; a job title *(doctor)*; the name of a thing *(radio)*; the name of a place *(London)*; the name of a quality *(courage)*; or the name of an action *(laughter)*.

1.2 Form of nouns [> Appendix 1]

Nouns may be single words like *desk*, or words we form with endings like *-er (player)*. We also form compound nouns from two or more words:

- adjective + noun: *a heavyweight, a redhead*
- gerund + noun: *drinking water, a frying pan*
- noun + gerund: *horse-riding, sight-seeing*
- noun + noun: in place of *of*: *a car key*
  place: *a town house*
  streets: *Oxford Street*
  material: *a cotton blouse*
  'types': *a horror film*
  containers: *a coffee pot*

1.3 Types of nouns

There are two types of nouns:

1 Proper nouns, which are the names of particular people *(Andrew)*, places *(America)* or unique things like *Monday, April* or *Christmas*. We spell proper nouns with capital letters and don't normally use *a/an* or *the* in front of them.

2 Common nouns, which fall into two groups:
   - **countable nouns**, which we use with *a/an* or in the plural: *a book, an envelope, three stamps*. We ask *How many*: **How many eggs** *are there?*
   - **uncountable nouns**, which we use without *a/an* and which don't have a plural: *sugar, milk*. We ask *How much*: **How much sugar** *is there?*

1.4 Countable and uncountable nouns

We need to know whether nouns are countable or uncountable so that we can tell when to use *a/an, the* or no article at all and when to use quantity words like *a few, a little, many* or *much.*

1.4.1 Nouns not normally countable in English [> App 2]

Some nouns are countable in other languages, but not in English. For example: *baggage, furniture, information, machinery, money, spaghetti.* This means we can't use them with *a/an* or in the plural:

> *I'd like **some information** please.* (Not **an**)

1.4.2 Partitives: 'a piece of' [> App 3]

Partitive suggests 'a part of something' to refer to:
- one item: *a **loaf** of bread, a **ball** of string.*
- part of a whole: *a **piece** of chalk, a **slice** of bread.*
- collections: *a **tin** of biscuits*; pairs: *a **pair** of shoes.*

Partitives go with some words, but not with others, so we can say *a **slice** of bread*, but not **a slice of soap**; *a piece of* combines with many nouns.

1.5 Number (singular and plural)

1.5.1 Regular plurals

We form the regular plural by adding:
-s to most nouns: *cat - cat**s**; cake - cake**s**.*
-es to most nouns ending in *-o (potato**es**), -s (class**es**), -x (box**es**), -ch (watch**es**), -sh (bush**es**).*
-ies to nouns which end in consonant + *y* in the singular: *coun**try** - count**ries**.*

1.5.2 Irregular plurals

- *man/men, woman/women, child/children, goose/ geese, foot/feet, mouse/mice, tooth/teeth.*
- some nouns ending in *-f* or *-fe: knife/knives, leaf/ leaves, life/lives, shelf/shelves, wife/wives.*
- same singular and plural: *deer, salmon, sheep.*
- foreign plurals: *medium/media, analysis/analyses.*

1.6 Gender (masculine or feminine)

In many languages, the names of things such as *book, chair, radio, table* may be grammatically masculine, feminine or neuter. Often gender doesn't relate to sex, so that the word for 'girl' might be neuter and the word for 'chair' might be feminine. There is no grammatical gender for English nouns. We use *he* and *she* to refer to people and *it* to refer to everything else. With most nouns referring to people, we don't know if the person referred to is male or female unless we hear or read a pronoun:

> ***My accountant*** *says **he** is moving **his** office.*
> ***My doctor*** *says **she** is pleased with my progress.*

'People nouns' are unisex, for example: *cook, friend, guest, journalist, neighbour, person, pupil, relative, scientist, student, teacher, tourist, writer.*

A few nouns have masculine and feminine varieties when they refer to sex: *man/woman, boy/girl, bull/cow.* A few feminine *-ess* endings survive, e.g. *waiter/ waitress*, but adding *-ess* to words like *author* is now old-fashioned. We often use *person* to refer to either sex: *the person who ...*, rather than *the man/woman who ... .*

The genitive

1.7 The use of the genitive in English

The only 'case form' for nouns in English is the possessive or genitive case (e.g. *man's, woman's*). This has limited uses in the modern language.

We add *apostrophe s ('s)* or *s apostrophe (s')* to nouns to show possession mainly by people, not by things. The spelling rule is:
Add *'s* to any personal noun unless it is in the form of a plural ending in *-s*, in which case, just add an apostrophe ('). For details, see **1.8** overleaf.

1.8 Form of the genitive

Add the following to *personal* nouns:

's to singular nouns:	*child*	+ *'s*:	*child's*
's to singular nouns ending in *-s*:	*actress*	+ *'s*:	*actress's*
's to the plural of irregular nouns:	*children*	+ *'s*:	*children's*
' to the plural of nouns ending in *-s*:	*girls*	+ *'*:	*girls'*
's to some names ending in *-s*:	*James*	+ *'s*:	*James's*

Examples: *a child's dream, an actress's career, children's games, a girls' school, James's brother.*
A genitive on its own can mean 'a shop': *the butcher's.*

1.9 'Possession' by things

If we want to show the 'genitive' of a thing, we may sometimes use *of (the key of the car)*, but in most cases we use a compound noun *(the car key)*. We form such compounds easily in English: *the kitchen door, a table leg, the water supply.*

1.10 'Possession' by things using 'of'

There are some fixed phrases with *of* where it isn't possible to form compound nouns. For example:
- parts of things: *the book of the film, the shade of a tree, the top/bottom/side/inside/outside of a box.*
- abstract: *the cost of living, the price of success.*

1.11 *'s* and *s'* with non-living things

There are some fixed phrases with *'s/s'* where we can't form compound nouns and where we often avoid using *of*. For example:
- time references: *a day's work* (*'s*: singular), *two days' work* (*s'*: plural).
- places called after people: *St Paul's, Macy's Store.*
- phrases: *the earth's surface, journey's end.*

1.12 The double genitive

We can't use *this* and *my* together in front of a noun. We have to say *this son of mine*, not **this my son**. We also use *'s* after *of* in expressions like *a friend of my father's, a play of Shakespeare's.*

2 Articles

The indefinite article: 'a/an'

2.1 Basic uses

There is no difference between *a* and *an*. We use:
- *a* before a consonant <u>sound</u>: *a fire, a hot dinner*.
- *an* before a vowel <u>sound</u>: *an umbrella, an honour*.
We use *a/an*:
- with singular countable nouns: *a book, an egg*.
- with an indefinite meaning, suggesting 'I can't/ won't tell you which', 'it doesn't matter which':
    *I'd like **an apple** please.* (it doesn't matter which)
- when we mention something for the first time:
    *I looked up and saw **a plane*** (first mention). ***The plane** flew low over the trees* (now you know which plane I mean).

2.2 Specific uses: singular and plural

2.2.1 Classification, identification

We use *a/an* to classify or identify people and things, as if we were 'labelling':
    *She's **a doctor**. It's **a book**.* (Not **She's doctor.**)
The plural form has no article:
    *They're **doctors**. They're **books**.*

2.2.2 Quantity

We use *a/an* to refer to quantity:
    *I'd like **an apple** please.* (i.e. any one)
The plural of *a/an* is *some* when we refer to quantity. (The exact number is not important.):
    *I'd like **some apples** please.*

2.3 'One' and 'a/an'

We don't normally use *one* in place of *a/an*. We use *one* when we are counting:
    *It was **one coffee** I ordered and not **two**.*
    *I've ordered **a coffee**.* ('any one', not specified)

The definite article: 'the'

2.4 Basic uses

The never varies in form whether it refers to people or things, singular or plural: *the man, the woman, the book; the men, the women, the books.*
We use *the* for definite reference:

> *I looked up and saw **a plane*** (first mention). ***The plane** flew low over the trees* (now you know which plane I mean: the reference is definite).

The combines with all common nouns:

> *That's **the man/woman/book** I asked you about.*
> *They're **the men/women/books** I asked about.*
> ***The water** in this glass isn't fit to drink.*

2.5 Specific uses

2.5.1 The group as a whole

We use *the* with nouns that refer to a particular group as a whole:

- specific groups: ***The public** want better services.*
- nationalities: ***The Japanese** are industrious.*

2.5.2 Limited context

In a 'limited context' the listener or reader can understand that a specific person, place or thing is being referred to:

- people: *Who's at the door? - It's **the postman**.*
- places: *Where's Jenny? - She's at **the library**.*
- parts of the body: *Alcohol affects **the brain**.*
- things in a room: *Your coat's behind **the door**.*

2.6 Unique items: 'one of a kind'

We use *the* to refer to 'one of a kind', for example:

- *the earth, the sea, the sky, the sun, the moon.*
- institutions: *the United Nations, the World Bank.*
- public bodies: *the Government, the Police.*
- the press: *The Economist, The Times.*
- species: *the human race, the dinosaurs.*

The zero article (-)

2.7 Basic uses
We often use nouns without any article at all in English. We can't refer to this as 'the omission of the article', because nothing has been omitted! We must refer to it as the zero article (-), that is, something we use as actively as *a/an* or *the*.
We use the zero article:
- with plural countable nouns: *beans*.
- with uncountable nouns, always singular: *water*.
- with proper nouns: *John*.

2.8 Zero article in general statements
Some languages use *the* in general statements where English uses zero. For example:
- plural countable nouns:
    (-) ***Beans*** *contain a lot of fibre.*
- uncountable nouns, whether concrete or abstract:
    (-) ***Water*** *boils at 100 °C.*
    (-) ***Life*** *is short;* (-) ***Art*** *is long.*

2.9 Zero article with proper nouns
We don't use *the* in front of names:
    (-) ***Elizabeth*** *is my mother's name.*
    (-) ***Mr and Mrs Jackson*** *are here to see you.*

2.10 Zero article with particular nouns
- days of the week, months: *See you on **Monday**.*
- meals: *Let's have **breakfast/lunch/tea/dinner**.*
- *school, hospital, bed, prison* when we refer to their purpose: *She's ill **in hospital**.* [> 7.2]
- transport: *I go everywhere **by bus**.*

2.11 Zero article or 'the' with place names
Place names are zero unless the first part is adjectival: *France, Italy, the USA; Rome, the Vatican City; Oxford Street, the British Museum; the Andes (Mountains); the Sahara (Desert).*

3 Pronouns

3.1 What is a pronoun?
A pronoun is a word like *he, she* or *it* that we use in place of a noun, as the word itself tells us: 'pro-noun'. We use pronouns when we already know who or what is referred to:

Jane *arrived late.* **She** *had had a long journey.*

3.2 Personal pronouns
These are:

subject:	*I*	*you*	*he*	*she*	*it*	*one*	*we*	*you*	*they*
object:	*me*	*you*	*him*	*her*	*it*	*one*	*us*	*you*	*them*

'Personal' refers to 'grammatical persons':
1st: *I, we*; 2nd: *you* (English doesn't distinguish between singular and plural *you*); 3rd: *he, she, it, one, they*. The 3rd person singular pronoun, not the noun, tells us whether a reference is masculine, feminine or neuter, singular or plural. People are *he, she* or *they*; everything else is *it* or *they* [> 1.6]:

Sandra *is here.* **She** *can't stay long.*
John and Sandra *are here.* **They** *can't stay long.*

Animals are usually *it*, unless they are pets, etc.:

What kind of dog is **Spot**? - **He's** *a mongrel.*

3.2.1 Subject and object pronouns
<u>Subject</u> pronouns come before a verb:

John *didn't find us in, so* **he** *left a message.*

<u>Object</u> pronouns come after verbs or prepositions:

Have you ever met **Marilyn**? - *I've never met* **her**.
I really feel sorry **for them**.

Object pronouns may also be indirect [> 16.4*n*.4]:

Give my regards **to him**.   *Give* **him** *my regards.*

We normally use object pronouns after *be*:

It's **me/him/her/us/them.** (rather than *It's I*, etc.)

We also use them in short answers:

Who wants a ride on my bike? - **Me!/Not me!**

3.3 One

3.3.1 'You' and 'one' as indefinite pronouns

We normally use *you* to make general statements:

> **You** (= anyone) *can't wash without soap.*

We may use *one* in place of *you* in formal language:

> *Things are better, but* **one** *can't expect miracles.*

3.3.2 'One' and 'ones' as 'prop words'

We don't normally use an adjective on its own as if it were a noun, so we can't say:

> *What colour car did you get? - *I got a red.**

We have to 'support' or 'prop up' the adjective, so we use *one* or *ones* to replace a countable noun:

> *What colour car did you get? - * **A red one**.

We often use *one/ones* after *Which*:

> **Which one(s)** *do you like? - I like* **the red one(s)**.

3.4 It

Important uses of *it* are:

- as an 'empty' subject: ***It's** hot.* (Not ***Is hot.**)

We need *it* here, because every English sentence must have a subject and verb.

- after verbs that need an object:

> *Do you like fish? - Yes, I like* ***it**.* (Not **I like.**)

- to avoid beginning sentences with *-ing* or *to* [> 15.13]:

> ***It's** pleasant **meeting/to meet old friends**.*

3.5 Possessive adjectives/possessive pronouns

These are:

adjectives:	my	your	his	her	its	our	your	their
pronouns:	mine	yours	his	hers	-	ours	yours	theirs

Possessive adjectives refer to the possessor, not the thing possessed. We use them before nouns:

> ***Ann** phones **her father** daily.* (= her own father)

We use possessive pronouns on their own:

> *These children are* **mine**. *(These are* **my children**.)

3.6 Reflexive pronouns
These are:

singular:	*myself*	*yourself*	*himself, herself, itself, oneself*
plural:	*ourselves*	*yourselves*	*themselves*

Important uses are:
- after verbs like *amuse, blame, cut, enjoy, hurt*:
    I **enjoyed myself** at the party. (Not *enjoyed me*)
- after *dress, shave*, etc. to show conscious effort:
    *Polly can already **dress herself**.*
- for emphasis: **She herself** *said so/said so* **herself**.

3.7 Demonstrative adjectives and pronouns
These are *this, that, these* and *those*:

singular:	*this/that*	*boy*	*girl*	*tree*	*book*	*money*
plural:	*these/those*	*boys*	*girls*	*trees*	*books*	-

This and *these* may refer to something close:
    *Let me show you **this (photo)**.*
That and *those* may refer to something distant:
    *Look at **that (picture)**.*
This and *that* can also refer to a person:
    *Who's **this/that**? (But not *Who are these/those? *)*

3.8 Indefinite pronouns
These are compounds of *some, any, no*, and *every*:

some-	any-	no-	every-
someone	*anyone*	*no one*	*everyone*
somebody	*anybody*	*nobody*	*everybody*
something	*anything*	*nothing*	*everything*

The rules for *some, any* and *no* apply [> 4.3-4].
We also use indefinite pronouns with:
- adjectives: *This is **something special**.*
                          *This isn't **anything important**.*
- comparatives: *I want **something cheaper**.*
- the *to*-infinitive: *Haven't you got **anything to do**?*

10

4 Quantity

4.1 Quantifiers: what they are and what they do

Quantifiers are numbers, or words like *some, a few, plenty of*. They show how many things or how much of something we are talking about. Some quantifiers combine with countable nouns; some with uncountable and some with both kinds:

+ plural	+ uncountable	+ plural + uncountable	+ singular countable
both books	*a bit of bread*	*some books* *some ink*	*each book*
both	a bit of	some (of the)	each
a few	a little	any (of the)	any/some (of the)
(not) many	(not) much	a lot of/lots of	every

4.2 Degrees of quantity

References to quantity can be definite:
>We need **six eggs** and **half a kilo** of butter.

Most quantifiers are indefinite. The most common, *some* and *any*, refer to quantity in general:
>Are there **any eggs**? Is there **any milk**?
>There are **some eggs**/There's **some milk** here.
>(= I don't know how many/how much.)

Not any and *no* show complete absence:
>There **aren't any** eggs. There **isn't any** milk.
>There **are no** eggs. There**'s no** milk.

Other quantity words give 'a rough idea':

plurals	uncountable nouns
approximately **how many**:	approximately **how much**:
There are **too many** eggs.	There is **too much** milk.
plenty of eggs.	**plenty of** milk.
a lot of/lots of eggs.	**a lot of/lots of** milk.
(not) enough eggs.	**(not) enough** milk.
a few eggs.	**a little** milk.
very few eggs.	**very little** milk.
not many eggs.	**not much** milk.
hardly any eggs.	**hardly any** milk.

4.3 Basic uses of 'some' and 'any'
We use *some* in:
- the affirmative: *I want **some eggs***.
- questions inviting 'yes': *Do you want **some eggs**?*
- in offers/requests: *Shall I get **some tea**?*
- *some* = 'certain': ***Some people** believe anything.*
We use *any* in:
- the negative: *I don't want **any tea**.*
- uncertain questions: *Are there **any eggs**?*
- with *hardly*: *There are **hardly any** eggs.*
- *any* = 'every': ***Any fool** knows that.*

4.4 Basic uses of 'not any', 'no' and 'none'
We can use *no* + noun in place of *not any*:
> *There isn't any bread. There's **no bread**.*
> *There aren't any sweets. There are **no sweets**.*
We use *none* on its own as a pronoun:
> *Is there **any bread**? - No, **there's none**.*
> *Are there **any sweets**? - No, **there are none**.*

4.5 Basic uses of 'much', 'many' and 'a lot of'
We can use *much* and *many* with an object in a
negative sentence, but *a lot of* (informal *lots of*) is more
usual in affirmative sentences:
> *He hasn't much time. He hasn't many books.*
> (Not **He has much time/He has many books.**)
> *He has **a lot of time/a lot of books**.*
Affirmative general statements are possible beginning
with *much* and *many*:
> ***Much money** has been spent on motorways.*
> ***Many books** have been written about London.*

4.6 Basic uses of 'few', 'a few', 'little', 'a little'
We use *few/a few* with countables: *(a) few friends*; and
little/a little with uncountables: *(a) little time*.
Few and *little* are 'negative' (= hardly any):
> *She has **few friends/little time** for him.*
A few and *a little* are 'positive' (= some):
> *I've got **a few friends/a little time** to spare.*

4.7 Basic uses of 'both' and 'all'
We use *both* and *both the* (or *both my/these*, etc.) in
the same way to refer to two people or things:
  ***Both children/Both the** children are here.*
We use *all* + noun to refer to things in general:
  ***All children** like to play.*
We use *all the/my,* etc. for particular reference:
  ***All the children in our street** like to play.*

4.8 'All' compared with 'everyone'/ 'everything'
It's unusual to use *all* to mean 'all the people' or 'all the
things'. We prefer *everyone/everything*:
  ***Everyone** is here.* (rather than 'All are here')
  ***Everything** is ready.* (rather than 'All is ready')

4.9 'Each' compared with 'every'
Each suggests 'one by one', 'separately'; *every*
suggests 'all together'. We can often use *each* and
every in exactly the same way:
  ***Each child/Every child** was questioned.*
  ***Every child in the world** loves a good story.*
  (*each* is unlikely in general statements)
We also use *each* (not *every*) to end a sentence:
  *They received a present **each**.*

4.10 'Other', 'others' and 'another'
We use *other* + plural noun:
  *There are **other ways** of answering the question.*
We use *another* + singular noun:
  *There's **another way** of answering the question.*
We use *the others* to mean 'the rest':
  *Let's wait here for **the others**.*

4.11 'Either' and 'neither'
Either and *neither* refer to two people or things.
Either means 'one or the other':
  *Which pot will you use? - **Either** (of them).*
Neither means 'not one and not the other':
  *Which pot will you use? - **Neither** (of them).*

5 Adjectives

5.1 What an adjective is and what it does
An adjective describes the person, thing, etc. which a noun refers to. We use adjectives to say what a person, etc. is like or seems like:

> a **clever** woman, a **nice** day, **brown** hair.

5.2 Formation of adjectives [> App 4]
Adjectives may be single-syllable words like *tall*, or may be formed with:
- suffixes: *enjoy**able**, truth**ful**, **act**ive, fool**ish***.
- prefixes: ***un**interesting, **im**possible, **dis**agreeable*.

The *-ing* form of a verb can also function as an adjective: *bor**ing**, excit**ing**, interest**ing**, tir**ing***.
Adjectives can also be compounds, for example:

> *a self-employed author, a three-year-old building.*

5.3 Basic uses of adjectives
- They do not vary in form to 'agree' with nouns:
  > a **tall** man/woman/tree, **tall** men/women/trees.
- They come before a noun or after *be, seem*, etc.:
  > A **young man** came in.
  >
  > John **is young/a young man**.
- They aren't used as if they were nouns:
  > You **poor thing**!   I'd like the **red one**.
- Some combine with *very, too* or *enough*:
  > **very** tall, **too** small, big **enough**.
- Some cannot combine with *very*, etc.:
  > He is **dead**. It is **unique**. (Not *very dead*, etc.)

5.4 Nouns that behave like adjectives
Combinations like the following are compound nouns [> 1.2]:

> *a cotton blouse, a gold watch, a plastic raincoat.*

A gold watch is a watch made of *gold*. In *a golden sunset, golden* is an adjective (= 'like gold').
Compare: *a silk blouse/silky hair, a stone wall/stony silence; a silver tray/the silvery moon.*

5.5 Adjectives after 'seem', 'look', 'feel', etc.
We use adjectives, not adverbs after *seem*, etc.:
>*She **seems nice**. It **looks awful**. I **feel happy**.*
>(Not **seems nicely**, etc.) Compare:
>*You **look well**. (well*, adjective = in good health)
>*You **play well**. (well*, an adverb telling us 'how')

5.6 Adjectives ending in '-ed' and '-ing' [> App 5]
We use some past participles ending in *-ed* (e.g. *excited*) and some present participles ending in *-ing* (e.g. *exciting*) as adjectives. Some common pairs are: *bored/boring, tired/tiring, interested/interesting*.

We often use *-ed* endings to describe people:
>*John* was **interested** *in the story.*

We often use *-ing* endings to refer to things, etc.:
>*The story* was **interesting**.

We can also use *-ing* endings to refer to people:
>*Cathy* is **interesting/an interesting person**.

5.7 'The' + adjective [> App 6]
We must use a noun after *the/a/an* + adjective:
>*He's **old**. He's **an old man**.* (Not **He's an old.**)

The plural forms are:
>*They're **old**. They're **old men**.* (Not **olds**)

We can use *the* + some adjectives to refer to 'the group as a whole', e.g. *the old, the blind, the rich*:
>*The old don't like change.* (Not **the olds**)

5.8 Nationality adjectives and nouns [> App 7]
When referring to nationalities, we prefer adjectival forms to nouns:
>*He's/She's **Japanese**.* (preferable to *a Japanese*)
>*He's/She's **Italian**.* (preferable to *an Italian*)
>*He's/She's **American**.* (preferable to *an American*)
>*He's/She's **Turkish**.* (preferable to *a Turk*)
>*He's/She's **English**.* (Not **an English**)
>*He's/She's **French**.* (Not **a French**)

5.9 Adjective word order

Adjectives used together are generally in this order:
'opinion'l sizel agel shapel colourl originl '-ed/-en'.
So we can have combinations like: *a lovely big smile, a large round table, a big blue flag, beautiful Italian shoes, delicious fresh home-made bread.*

5.10 The comparison of adjectives

5.10.1 Form

Shorter adjectives (not more than two syllables)

adjective	comparative	superlative
clean	*clean**er***	*clean**est***
big	*big**ger***	*big**gest***
nice	*nice**r***	*nice**st***
narrow	*narrow**er***	*narrow**est***

Some adjectives like *narrow* (e.g. *clever, pleasant*) can also form their comparative and superlative with *more/most: more/most narrow.*

Irregular adjectives

good	*better*	*best*
bad	*worse*	*worst*
much/many	*more*	*most*
little	*less*	*least*

Longer adjectives and -ed/-ing forms

attractive	*more attractive*	*most attractive*
attractive	*less attractive*	*least attractive*
bored/boring	*more/less bored/boring*	*most/least bored/boring*

5.10.2 Use of the comparative and superlative

We use the comparative form when comparing one person or thing with another:

> *Jane's **taller than** Pam. Pam's **not as tall as** Jane.*

We use the superlative form when we are comparing one person or thing with more than one other in the same group:

> *This is **the cleanest** room in the house.*
> *This is **the best/the worst** hotel in town.*
> *The last question was **the most difficult** of all.*

6 Adverbs

6.1 What an adverb is and what it does

An adverb (ad-verb) adds to the meaning of a verb by telling us *how*, *when*, *where*, etc. Adverbs can be single words (for example, *badly*) or phrases (for example, *in the park*):

> He drives **badly**. (How does he drive?)
> They played **in the park**. (Where did they play?)

6.2 The comparison of adverbs

Most adverbs use *more* in the comparative: *more easily*, and *most* in the superlative: *most easily*.
Irregular comparisons are:

well	*better*	*best*;	*badly*	*worse*	*worst*;
much	*more*	*most*;	*little*	*less*	*least*.

6.3 Adverbs of manner [> App 8]

Adverbs of manner tell us *how* something happens. We form them by adding *-ly* or *-ily* to an adjective:

slow   slowly; *heavy   heavily*:
> It was a **slow** train.   It went **slowly**.
> It was **heavy** rain.   It rained **heavily**.

Some adverbs have the same form as adjectives:
> It was a **fast** train. It went **fast**.

Some of these, e.g. *hard, high, last, late* and *near* also have an *-ly* form with a different meaning:
> We got the **late** bus. (adjective)
> The bus ran **late**. (adverb)
> We haven't been out a lot **lately**. (= recently)

Some have two forms used in the same way:
> I bought it **cheap**. I bought it **cheaply**.

Some adjectives end in *-ly* but cannot be used as adverbs: *cowardly, friendly, lively, lovely, silly*:
> Meg is a **friendly** girl.
> Meg greeted me **in a friendly way**.
> (Not *Meg greeted me friendly.*)

6.4 Adverbs of time [> App 31]

Adverbs of time tell us *when* something happens. They are usually 'points of time' like *today, yesterday, last week, this morning, on Monday*:

> I saw Lucy **this morning/yesterday/on Monday**.

Other adverbs of time:
- *still* (= until now) to emphasize continuity:
  > I'm **still** waiting for my new passport.
- *yet* (= until now) at the end of sentences:
  > Has your new passport arrived **yet**? (question)
  > My new passport has**n't** arrived **yet**. (negative)
- *already* (= before now, so soon):
  > I've **already** seen the film. I've seen it **already**.
  > Has he **already** gone? Has he gone **already**?

6.5 Adverbial phrases of duration

Adverbial phrases of duration tell us *how long* an action continues. We form them with:
- *since* + exact time reference:
  > I haven't seen him **since January**.
- *for* + period of time:
  > We've lived here **for three years**.
- *during* and *in*:
  > We had a lot of fun **during/in the holidays**.
- *by* (= not later than); *till* (= not before):
  > She'll arrive **by 5 o'clock**.
  > She **won't** arrive **till 5 o'clock**.

6.6 Adverbs of frequency [> App 9]

These are adverbs like *always, usually, frequently, often* and *sometimes* which answer *How often?* They have three basic positions:
- after *be* when it's the only verb in a sentence:
  > I'm **always** late.
- after the first auxiliary if there's more than one:
  > I could **never** have succeeded without your help.
- before the main verb when there's only one verb:
  > She **often** goes to London on Fridays.

6.7 Adverbs of degree [> App 10]

These are adverbs like *quite, fairly* and *rather*, which often combine with adjectives. Vocal stress makes the meaning stronger or weaker:

*The film is **quite good**.*
(stress on *good* = better than I expected)
*The film is **quite good**.*
(stress on *quite* = less than the maximum)

- *fairly* goes with 'good' adjectives:
*The film is **fairly good**.*
- *rather* means 'inclined to be' (good or bad):
*His work has been **rather poor**.*
- *much, far, a lot* (for comparisons):
*This flat's **much/far/a lot bigger** than our old one.*

6.8 Intensifiers [> App 11]

Intensifiers are words like *very* and *too* which strengthen adjectives and adverbs:

*Lydia is **nice**.   Lydia is **very nice**.*

Too + adjective means 'more than is desirable'. Compare *very* and *too*:

*This coffee is **very hot*** (but I can drink it).
*This coffee is **too hot*** (so I can't drink it).

We can use *-ly* adverbs like *extremely* and *really* for special emphasis in place of *very*:

*I'm **extremely sleepy**.*

6.9 Focus adverbs

We use adverbs like *even* and *only* to 'focus' attention on the word(s) we want to emphasize:

***Even/Only** I understood Professor Boffin.*

Too at the end of a sentence means 'also':

*I understood Professor Boffin, **too**.*

This becomes *not ... either* in the negative:

*I did**n't** understand Professor Boffin, **either**.*

6.10 Viewpoint adverbs [> App 12]

Adverbs like *briefly, naturally* express a viewpoint:

***Naturally**, I agree with you.*

7 Prepositions and adverb particles

7.1 Prepositions and adverb particles [> App 13]
There are many 'small words' in English, such as *up,
down* and *by* which we call prepositions. In fact, we use
most of these words as prepositions or as adverb
particles. A preposition must have an object (a noun or
a pronoun like *me, him*):

> **across** the road, **over** the wall, **up** the hill.
> It's **for you and me**. (Not **for you and I*)

An adverb particle doesn't need an object; it adds to the
meaning of the verb:

> walk **across**, drive **over**, come **up**, climb **down**.

Prepositions express relationships:

> I bought this **for Jim**. I gave it **to him**.

They may take the form of:
- single words: *at, from, in, to, into*, etc.
- two or more words: *according to, apart from*, etc.

7.2 Prepositions of direction and position [> App 14]
We use *to/from* and *into/out of* to show movement:

> She's gone **to**/come **from Paris**.
> She went **into**/came **out of the shop**.

We use *at, in, on* to show position after movement: **at** a
point, **in** an area, **on** a surface (**on** the table):

> I'll meet you **at the airport**. (= a meeting point)
> I'll meet you **in the airport**. (= inside the building)

Similarly: *at/in the cinema, the office, the bank*.

to/at: He's gone **to a party**. He's **at a party**.
- places: *to/at the airport, the bank, the butcher's*.
- 'attend': *to/at church, school, college, university*.
- events: *to/at a concert, a dance, a meeting*.

to/in: She's gone **to Paris**. She's **in Paris**.
- large areas/towns: *to/in Europe, Texas, London*.
- 'outside': *to/in the garden, the park, the square*.
- *to/in bed, church, prison, the kitchen*.

7.3 Prepositions of time: 'at', 'on' and 'in'

at: exact time: *at 10 o'clock*; meal times: *at lunch time*; points of time: *at night*; festival-time: *at New Year*; age: *at the age of 14*.

on: days of the week: *on Monday*; parts of the day: *on Monday morning*; dates: *on June 1st*; birthdays: *on your birthday*.

in: parts of the day: *in the evening*; months: *in May*; years: *in 2050*; seasons: *in (the) spring*; centuries: *in the 21st century*.

7.4 Other prepositions of movement, place and time

Some prepositions show movement or lack of movement depending on the verbs they follow:
> The air balloon **flew above** the city.
> The air balloon **was above** the city.

7.4.1 Movement [> App 13]

Prepositions with 'movement verbs' (e.g. *run*):
run *across* the road; run *after* a bus; walk *along* the path; walk *beside* me; drive *behind* me; put *into*/take *out of* a box; drive *over/under* a bridge.

7.4.2 Position/place [> App 13]

Prepositions with 'position verbs' (e.g. *be*):
the room *above* the kitchen; the car parked *behind* mine; the building *beside/next to* my house; stand *between* two trees; *near/a long way from/not far from* my house; the building *opposite* the station.

7.4.3 Time

These prepositions refer to time:
(at) about 10 o'clock; *after/before* lunch; we're open *from* 9 *to/till* six; *around* 6 in the evening; *between* 6 and 7 this evening; be home *by* 6; *during* the afternoon; *in* the morning; *on* Wednesday; *since* last year; *till/until* tomorrow.

7.5 Phrasal verbs

We often combine verbs with prepositions and adverb particles to form phrasal verbs. These verbs can have non-idiomatic or idiomatic meanings. We use them a lot. So, for example, if someone knocks at the door, we would probably say 'Come in', rather than 'Enter'. We can define four types:

Type 1: verb + preposition + object: *Listen to this!*
Type 2: verb + particle + object: *Take off your hat.*
Type 3: verb + particle (no object): *Hurry up!*
Type 4: verb + particle + preposition: *put up with.*

7.5.1 Type 1: verb + preposition + object [> Apps 15-17]

<u>non-idiomatic</u>: I *agree with* you; I *depend on* you; I *suffer from* asthma; I *insist on* paying, etc.
<u>non idiomatic</u>: <u>verb + object + preposition + object</u>:
accuse me of lying; *explain this to* me, etc.
<u>idiomatic</u>: it *went for* me (= attacked); *sleep on* it
(= decide later); don't *stand for* it (= tolerate), etc.

7.5.2 Type 2: verb + particle + object [> Apps 18-19]

The particle strengthens or extends the meaning of a verb. We can separate the particle from the verb:

He **took off** his hat.   He **took** his hat **off**.
He **took it off**. (Not **He took off it.**)

<u>non-idiomatic</u>: *put (out)* your hand *(out)*; *write (down)* my address *(down)*; *chop (up)* that wood *(up)*; *cut (down)* that tree *(down)*, etc.
<u>idiomatic</u>: *bring (out)* your article *(out)* (= publish); *call (up)* your mother *(up)* (= telephone), etc.

7.5.3 Type 3: verb + particle (no object) [> App 20]

<u>non-idiomatic</u>: *hurry up*; *sit down*; *stand up*, etc.
<u>idiomatic</u>: she *broke down* (= collapsed); *mind out* (= be careful); things *are looking up* (= improving).

7.5.4 Type 4: verb + particle + preposition [> App 21]

<u>non-idiomatic</u>: *drive on to* Oxford, etc.
<u>idiomatic</u>: don't *put up with* it (= tolerate).

8 Verbs, verb tenses, imperatives

8.1 What a verb is and what it does

A verb is a word *(run)* or a phrase *(run out of)* which expresses the doing of an action *(take, play)* or the existence of a state *(love, seem)*. We also use verbs to express distinctions in time (past, present and future) through tenses.

8.2 Verb tenses, simple and progressive

English has only two tense forms: present *(love, write)* and past *(loved, wrote)*. We have to 'make up' other tenses with auxiliary verbs: e.g. *have* + past participle to form the present perfect. Tenses give only a general idea of when an action takes place since, in English, tense and time are only loosely related. All tenses have two aspects: simple and progressive. The progressive adds to the simple by telling us that an action is/was, etc. in progress:

	simple	progressive	
present:	I work.	I am	working.
past:	I worked.	I was	working.
present perfect:	I have worked.	I have been	working.
past perfect:	I had worked.	I had been	working.
future:	I will work.	I will be	working.
future perfect:	I will have worked.	I will have been	working.

8.3 Dynamic and stative verbs [> App 22]

Dynamic verbs refer to deliberate actions *(I'm writing)*. Stative verbs refer to states we can't control *(I see very well)*. There are three classes:
- dynamic verbs, which can be simple or progressive:
    I often **listen** to records. *I'm* **listening** to one now.
- stative verbs, which can be only simple:
    This coat **belongs** to you. (Not *is belonging**)
- verbs that have different dynamic or stative uses:
    I'm **weighing** myself. (= that's what I'm doing)
    I **weigh** 65 kilos. (i.e. a state)

8.4 The present tense

simple present	present progressive
We add -s or -es to the base form of the verb after *he*, *she* and *it*:	We form the progressive with *am/is/are* + -*ing*. [> 9.1]

I	work		
You	work		
He/She/It	work**s**	hard.	
We	work		
They	work		

I'm	
You're	*waiting.*
He's/She's/It's	*writing.*
We're	*beginning.*
They're	*running.*

8.4.1 Main uses of the simple present tense
- permanent truths: *Gases **expand** when heated.*
- 'the present period':   *My mother **wears** glasses.*
- habitual actions: *John **travels** a lot.*
- with future reference: *Our friends **arrive** tonight.*

8.4.2 Main uses of the present progressive
- actions in progress now: *He**'s waiting** for a bus.*
- temporary situations: *Nina**'s studying** English.*
- planned future actions: *We**'re leaving** tomorrow.*

8.5 The past tense [> back cover for regular/irregular verbs]

simple past	past progressive
The form is the same in all persons:	We form the progressive with *was/were* + -*ing*. [> 9.2]

I	
You	
He/She/It	*worked hard.* (regular)
We	*went out.* (irregular)
They	

I was	
You were	
He/She/It was	*waiting.*
We were	
They were	

8.5.1 Main use of the simple past tense [> App 31]
- actions which happened in the past and finished; we always say, or imply, *when*:
   *This letter **arrived this morning**.*

8.5.2 Main uses of the past progressive
- temporary past actions: *It **was raining** last night.*
- + *when/as/just as*: *He arrived **as we were leaving**.*

8.6 The present perfect tense [> back cover for verbs]

simple present perfect	present perfect progressive
We form the present perfect with	We form the progressive with
have/has + a past participle [> 9.8]:	*have been* + *-ing* [> 9.3]:
I've worked	*I've been*
You've worked	*You've been*
He/She/It's worked hard.	*He's/She's/It's been* ⎰ *working.*
We've worked	*We've been*
They've worked	*They've been*

8.6.1 Main uses of the simple present perfect tense

1 actions beginning in the past and continuing to now:
- with *so far/ever/never*:   *I've never eaten papaya.*
- with *since* + time: *I've lived here since 1992.*
- with *for* + period: *I've lived here for years.*

2 actions without an exact time reference:
- 'at any time':   *Have you seen the Mona Lisa?*
- with *just*:   *I've just swept the kitchen.*
- with *already*:   *I've already had breakfast.*

8.6.2 Main use of the present perfect progressive
- unfinished actions: *I've been painting this room.*
(Compare: *I've painted this room*: a finished action.)

8.7 The past perfect tense

simple past perfect	past perfect progressive
We form the past perfect with	We form the progressive with
had + a past participle [> 9.8]:	*had been* + *-ing* [> 9.4]:
I/You/He/She/It/We/They	*I/You/He/She/It/We/They*
had finished.	*had been working all day.*

8.7.1 Main uses of the past perfect
- first of two events: *When I arrived, Ann had left.*
- optional use: *After I (had) finished, I left.*

8.7.2 Main use of the past perfect progressive
- unfinished actions during an 'earlier past':
    I was tired. I had been painting my room.
    (Compare: *I'd painted my room*: a finished action.)

8.8 The future tense [> App 31]

simple future	future progressive
We form the simple future with *will/ shall* and the base form of the verb:	We form the progressive with *will/shall be + -ing* [> 9.4]:
I'll/I will/I shall ⎫	*I'll/I will/I shall be*
You'll/You will ⎪	*You'll/You will be*
He'll/She'll/It'll (will) ⎬ stay.	*He'll/She'll/It'll be* *waiting.*
We'll/We will/We shall ⎪	*We'll/We will/We shall be*
They'll/They will ⎭	*They'll/They will be*

Notes: *Will* abbreviates to *'ll* ; the negative is *won't*.
We may use *shall/shan't* in place of *will/won't* after *I/We*.

8.8.1 Main uses of the simple future
- prediction: **It'll (It will) rain** tomorrow.
- sudden decision: **I'll stop** for some petrol.
- announcements: The wedding **will take place** soon.

8.8.2 Main uses of the future progressive
- 'imagining': Tomorrow **I'll be lying** on a beach!
- to sound more polite: **I'll be seeing** you tomorrow.
- planned events: **We'll be leaving** tomorrow.

8.9 The future perfect tense

future perfect simple	future perfect progressive
We form the future perfect simple *will/shall have* + a past participle:	We form the progressive with *will/shall have been + -ing*:
I'll/I will/shall ⎫	*I'll/I will/shall have been*
You'll/You will ⎪	*You'll/You will have been*
He'll/She'll/It'll ⎬ have done it by...	*He'll/She'll/It'll have been eating.*
We'll/We will/shall ⎪	*We'll/We will/shall have been*
They'll/They will ⎭	*They'll/They will have been*

8.9.1 Main use of the future perfect tense
- actions already completed by a time in the future:
  Claire **will have retired** by the year 2020.

8.9.2 Main use of the future perfect progressive
- what is now in progress from a future viewpoint:
  By May 1st I **will have been teaching** for 24 years.

8.10 The 'going to'-future

We form the *going to*-future with *am/is/are going to* + the base form of the verb:

I'm/You're/He's/She's/It's/We're/They're going to arrive tomorrow.

8.10.1 Main uses of the 'going to'-future
- response to 'a sign' of something about to happen:
  Look at those clouds! It's going to rain.
- firm intentions:
  I'm going to stay at home this evening.

8.11 Other ways of expressing the future
- *I am to, You are to*, etc. for formal duties:
  OPEC ministers are to meet in Geneva tomorrow.
- *It is due to*, etc. for timetables:
  Flight BA 561 is due to arrive at 13.15.
- *It is about to*, etc. for the immediate future:
  The race is about to start.
- present progressive: *We're leaving immediately.*
- simple present: *We leave tomorrow.*

8.12 The imperative

The imperative form is the same as the bare infinitive:

Affirmative (base form of the verb):	*Wait!*
Negative short form (*Don't* + base form):	*Don't wait!*
Emphatic form:	*Do wait a moment!*
Addressing someone:	*(You) wait here, Carol!*
Imperatives joined by *and*:	*Go and play outside.*

8.12.1 Main uses of the imperative
We use it not only for 'giving orders', but e.g. for:
- directions: *Take the 2nd turning on the right.*
- advice: *Don't worry!*
- warnings: *Look out! Take care!*
- instructions: *Use a moderate oven.*
- prohibitions: *Keep off the grass.*
- with *and*:   *Go and get a paper. Come and play. Wait and see.*
  (Not *Go to* *Come to*
  Wait to, but: *Try to/and*)

9 Be, Have, Do

'Be'

9.1 The simple present form of 'be'

affirmative full form				short form		negative short form		
		I	am		I'm	I'm	not =	-
		You	are		You're	You're	not = You	aren't
Tom	is	= He	is	Tom's	He's	He's	not = He	isn't
Ann	is	= She	is	Ann's	She's	She's	not = She	isn't
My bag	is	= It	is	My bag's	It's	It's	not = It	isn't
Tom and I	are	= We	are		We're	We're	not = We	aren't
Ann and you	are	= You	are		You're	You're	not = You	aren't
Tom and Ann	are	= They	are		They're	They're	not = They	aren't

(right brace) old.

9.2 The simple past form of 'be'

affirmative	negative full form	negative short form
I/He/She/It was	I/He/She/It was not	I/He/She/It wasn't
We/You/They were	We/You/They were not	We/You/They weren't

9.3 The present perfect form of 'be'

affirmative	short form	negative short form
I/You/We/They have been	I've/You've/We've/They've been	I/You/We/They haven't been
He/She/It has been	He's/She's/It's been	He/She/It hasn't been

9.4 Other forms

present and past progressive: *I*, etc. *am/was being careful.*
past perfect: *I*, etc. *had been*, etc.; **short form**: *I'd been*
future: *I*, etc. *will be*, etc.; (negative): *I won't be*

9.5 Main uses of 'be' as an auxiliary verb
Be 'helps' other verbs to form tenses: for example, the present or past progressive: *I **am/was** sleeping.*
Be + past participle forms passives: *It **was sold**.*

9.6 Main uses of 'be' as a full verb
- with nouns and adjectives: *I'm **a teacher**. I'm **tall**.*
- imperative: ***Be** careful. **Don't be** careless.*
- 'temporary behaviour': ***You're/You were being** silly.*
- *There + be*: ***There is/There was** a letter for you.*

'Have'

9.7 The present form of 'have got' (possession)

affirmative full form			short form			negative short form		
	I	*have got*		*I've*	*got*	*I*	*haven't got*	
	You	*have got*		*You've*	*got*	*You*	*haven't got*	
Tom	*= He*	*has got*	*Tom's*	*He's*	*got*	*He*	*hasn't got*	
Ann	*= She*	*has got*	*Ann's*	*She's*	*got*	*She*	*hasn't got*	*a chance.*
My car	*= It*	*has got*	*My car's*	*It's*	*got*	*It*	*hasn't got*	
Tom and I	*= We*	*have got*		*We've*	*got*	*We*	*haven't got*	
Ann and you	*= You*	*have got*		*You've*	*got*	*You*	*haven't got*	
Tom and Ann	*= They*	*have got*		*They've*	*got*	*They*	*haven't got*	

9.8 Form and uses of 'have' and 'have got'
- We use *have* and *have got* as stative verbs to show possession. There are no progressive forms:
> *Our dog* **has/has got** *long ears.* (Not **is having**)
- We use *have got* mainly in the present; otherwise we use *I had, I have had, I will have,* etc.:
> *I***'ve had** *this car for four years.* (Not **I had got**)
- We may use *have* as a full verb in place of *have got*, with the question forms *Do/Did you have* ...? and the negative forms: *I haven't/I hadn't* ... .
- *Have* also 'helps' other verbs to form tenses, for example, the present perfect: *I* **have eaten**.

9.9 'Have' to mean 'take', 'enjoy', etc. [> App 23]
We also use *have* as a dynamic verb with simple and progressive forms in the sense of 'eat, enjoy, experience, drink, take', etc.
Compare dynamic and stative uses:
> *I'***m having** *a drink.* (= I'm drinking)
> *I* **have/***I* **have got** *a drink.* (i.e. in my hand)
Some uses of *have* as a dynamic verb:
imperative: **Have** *a biscuit!*
simple present: **Do you have** *sugar?*
present progressive: **We're having** *a nice time.*
simple past: **We had** *a nice party last week.*
present perfect: **She's** *just* **had** *an accident!*
simple future: *I'll* **have** *a haircut tomorrow.*

'Do'

9.10 The simple present form of 'do'

affirmative		negative full form			negative short form		
I	do	I	do	not	I	don't	
You	do	You	do	not	You	don't	
He	does	He	does	not	He	doesn't	
She	does	She	does	not	She	doesn't	
It	does	the job.	It	does	not	It	doesn't	do the job.
We	do	We	do	not	We	don't	
You	do	You	do	not	You	don't	
They	do	They	do	not	They	don't	

Notes

The simple past of *do* is formed with *did* in all persons:
I, etc. *did, I did not, I didn't*.

The present perfect of *do* is formed with *have*:
I have/It has done, I haven't/It hasn't done.

9.11 Main uses of 'do' as an auxiliary verb

We use *do, does* and *did* to form questions and
negatives with full verbs, present and past:

> **Do** you drive? I **don't** drive.
> **Does** he drive? He **doesn't** drive.
> **Did** he phone? He **didn't** phone.

9.12 Main uses of 'do' as a full verb

- in the sense of 'work at':

> Who **does** the housework?

- to avoid repeating a previous verb:

> You **work** so hard. I don't know how you **do** it!

- for 'named tasks':

> I've **done the shopping/the ironing/the washing**.

9.13 'Do' and 'make' [> App 24]

Do and *make* combine with particular words:

do + *your best; business with someone; damage
to something; a favour; the washing*, etc.

make + *an accusation; an agreement; an
appointment; an arrangement; a bed*, etc.

10 Modal auxiliaries and related verbs

10.1 What modal auxiliaries are and what they do
Verbs like *can* and *may* are modal auxiliaries. We often refer to them as 'modal verbs' or 'modals'. We use them with other verbs, for example to ask for permission:
> ***May*** *I/****Can*** *I use your phone please?*

There are ten modal verbs: *can, could, may, might, will, would, shall, should, must* and *ought to*; and three 'semi-modals': *need, dare* and *used to*.

10.2 Important characteristics
- We use a bare infinitive after them, not 'to':
> *I **can see** you tomorrow.* (Not **can to see**)
- There is no *-(e)s* in the 3rd person singular:
> *The boss **can** see you now.* (Not **cans**)
- Questions/negatives are formed as for *be* [> 12.1-2]:
> ***Can he*** *come with us?* ***He can't*** *come with us.*

10.3 Two main uses of modal verbs
In their first use, modal verbs have dictionary meanings: e.g. *can/could* for ability; *may/might* for permission, but they aren't 'complete verbs' and we have to make up their 'missing parts'. For example, *must* can refer to the present or future:
> *I **must go now**. I **must go** back **tomorrow**.*

But to refer to the past we need *had to*:
> *I **had to go** to the bank **yesterday**.*

In their second use, we use nine modals (not *shall*) to express degrees of certainty or uncertainty. We express the greatest uncertainty with *might* and the greatest certainty with *must/can't* [> 10.8]:
> *He **might know** the answer.* (very uncertain)
> *He **must know** the answer.* (almost certain)

In this use, modals have only two forms:
- present: *He **must be** right.*
- perfect or past: *He **must have been** right.*

10.4 Expressing present and past ability

We use *can* or *am/is/are able to* to describe natural or learned ability:

> Jane **can run** fast. John **can dance** well.

We use *could* for general ability in the past:

> Jane **could run** fast when she was a girl.

We use *was/were able to* or *managed to* for the successful completion of an action in the past:

> I **was able to get**/I **managed to get** two tickets for tomorrow's match. (Not *could get*)

We use *can* (present) or *could* (past) for the senses:

> Cats **can see** very well in the dark.
> I **couldn't** quite **hear** what he said.

10.5 Asking for permission

We can ask for permission in four ways:
- with *Can*, which is very informal:

> **Can** I borrow your umbrella please?

- with *Could*, which is more polite than *Can*:

> **Could** I borrow your umbrella please?

- with *May*, which is more 'respectful':

> **May** I borrow your umbrella please?

- with *Might*, which is very polite, but not common:

> **Might** I borrow your umbrella please?

We can also precede such requests with *I wonder if* and *Do you think*: **I wonder if I might** trouble you?

10.6 Giving and refusing permission

We give and refuse permission with *can* and *may*:

> You **can('t)/may (not) stay up** till 9 o'clock.

To be more emphatic, we use *be allowed to*:

> You**'re allowed to/not allowed to smoke** here.

We express total prohibition with *mustn't*:

> You **mustn't smoke** here.

10.7 Past reference to permission

May and *must* are not 'complete verbs', so we use *was/were allowed to*, not *could*, for past reference:

> The children **were allowed to watch** TV last night.

10.8 Certainty and uncertainty

We can express degrees of certainty on a scale to refer to the present:

*They **are** at home.* (= it's a certain fact)
*They **could be** at home.* (= doubtful possibility)
*They **should be** at home.* (= doubtful possibility)
*They **may be** at home.* (allowing a possibility)
*They **might be** at home.* (less certain than *may*)

We can express degrees of certainty in the negative on a scale to refer to the present:

*They **aren't** at home.* (= it's a certain fact)
*They **can't be** at home.* (= it's nearly certain)
*They **couldn't be** at home.* (less certain than *can't*)
*They **may not be** at home.* (allowing a possibility)
*They **might not be** at home.* (less certain than *may*)

We express past degrees of certainty like this:

*They **were** at home.*
  *They **could have been** at home.* etc.
*They **weren't** at home.*
  *They **can't/couldn't have been** at home.* etc.

10.9 Deduction

We express deduction with *must be*, the negative of which is *can't be* (present); and *must have been*, the negative of which is *can't have been* (past):

*If she's eating, she **must be** better.*
*If she isn't eating, she **can't be** better.*
*If she was eating, she **must have been** better.*
*If she wasn't eating, she **can't have been** better.*

Compare *must/mustn't* to express obligation:

*You **must be** careful.*
*You **mustn't be** careless.* (Not **can't be**)
*It was dangerous, so I **had to be** careful.*
(Not *must have been*)
*It was a holiday, so I **didn't have to be** at work.*
(Not *can't have been*)

10.10 Offers, requests and suggestions

We use modals for the following social activities:

1 Offering things and substances:
> **Would/Wouldn't you like** a sandwich/some coffee?

2 Requesting things and substances:
> **Can/Could/May/Might I have** a sandwich/some sugar, please? [compare > 10.5]

3 Making suggestions, inviting actions:
> **Would/Wouldn't you like to** come with us?

4 Requesting others to do things for you:
> **Will/Would you** please **open** the door for me?

5 Offering to do things for others:
> **Shall I carry** that parcel for you?

6 Making suggestions that include the speaker:
> **Shall we go** for a swim?

10.11 Expressing wishes

We can express wishes with *I wish*, *If only* and *It's (about) time*. *If only* expresses more strongly the idea that the situation wished for cannot exist, whereas *wish* is also used for something that might happen. After *I wish*, etc. we 'go one tense back':

- the past refers to the present:
> **I wish I had** a better watch! (i.e. NOW)

- the past perfect refers to the past:
> **If only you had asked** me first. (i.e. THEN)

We may use *were* in all persons after *I wish*, etc.:
> I wish Tessa **was** here now. (informal)
> I wish Tessa **were** here now. (more formal)

We use *could* (ability), not *would* after *I* and *we*:
> I can't swim.   **I wish I could** swim.
> We weren't together.   **I wish we could have been** together!

Compare *would* after *I wish* to refer to willingness:
> **I wish he would** come tomorrow.
> **I wish you wouldn't** make so much noise.

10.12 Saying something is advisable

We use modals and other verbs to say that something is advisable. We can do this on a scale which shows the subjective view of the speaker:
- *should* (= in my opinion, it's advisable to):
    You **should see** a doctor.
- *ought to*, which may be slightly stronger:
    You **ought to vote**. (It's your public duty.)
- *had better*, stronger, carrying a warning:
    You**'d better drive** more carefully next time.
- *have to/must*, for inescapable obligation:
    You **must**/You **have to phone** home at once.

10.13 Saying something is inadvisable

We use modals and other verbs to say that something is inadvisable:
- *shouldn't* (= in my opinion, it isn't advisable to):
    You **shouldn't drink** so much coffee.
- *oughtn't to*, which may be slightly stronger:
    You **oughtn't to park** so near the corner.
- *had better not*, stronger, carrying a warning:
    You**'d better not overtake** here.
- *can't/mustn't* for absolute prohibition:
    You **can't/mustn't turn** left.

We can use either *needn't* or *don't have to* to mean 'it isn't necessary':
    I **needn't work**/I **don't have to work** tomorrow.
But in the past, there is a difference in meaning:
    I **needn't have gone** to work. (but I did)
    I **didn't have to go** to work. (and I didn't)

10.14 'Used to' for past habit

Used to is a simple past form only and refers to past habit. If we want to say 'I am in the habit of', we must use the simple present: I **get up** early. (Not *I use to get up early.*) We use *used to* to make a contrast between past and present:
    I **used to eat** a large breakfast. (but I don't now)

11 The passive and the causative

11.1 The passive

In the <u>active</u>, the subject does the action:

John burnt the dinner last night.

In the <u>passive</u>, the action is done to the subject:

The dinner was burnt last night.

We form the passive with *be* + past participle:

present: *he writes*   **it is written**
past: *he wrote*   **it was written**
modal: *he may write*   **it may be written**

We use the passive:
- when we don't want to take responsibility:
    The matter will be dealt with soon.
- to focus on 'what', rather than 'who':
    Our roof was damaged in last night's storm.
- to avoid 'vague subjects' like *one* or *someone*:
    The form **has to be signed**.

We use *by* + 'agent' only when we need to:

'Oliver Twist' was written **by Dickens**.

11.2 The causative

We form the causative with *have* + noun or pronoun object + past participle. Compare:

*I **had** a house **built**.* (causative)
*I **had built** a house.* (past perfect)

We use the causative to stress the fact that we are 'causing' someone to do a job for us:

*I **had** my car **serviced**.* (Not **I serviced my car.**)
*I must **have** my hair **cut**.* (Not **cut my hair**)

We often use the causative with verbs like *build, clean, decorate, mend, print, repair, service*.

We sometimes use *get* in place of *have* to show that we 'pressed' for something to be done:

*I finally **got** my roof **repaired**.* (i.e. with difficulty)

12 Questions, answers, negatives

12.1 Yes/No questions and Yes/No answers

We derive Yes/No questions from statements. In the case of *be, have* and modal verbs like *can* and *must*, we do this by inversion, that is by putting *be, have* or *can*, etc. in front of the subject:

She is *leaving.*   **Is she** *leaving?*
He can *drive a bus.*   **Can he** *drive a bus?*

With all other verbs, we form Yes/No questions with *Do* and *Does* in the simple present and *Did* in the simple past. They go in front of the subject. The form of the verb is always the bare infinitive:

We turn *left here.*   **Do we turn** *left here?*
He works *well.*   **Does he work** *well?*
They arrived *late.*   **Did they arrive** *late?*

When answering with *Yes* or *No*, we usually repeat the first part of the question:

Was he *late? -* Yes, **he was.***/No,* **he wasn't***.*
Can he *play chess? -* Yes, **he can.***/No,* **he can't***.*
We don't just answer 'Yes' or 'No', which can sound rude. Note **Are you** *...? -* Yes, **I am***.*

12.2 Negative statements

When a sentence contains *be, have* or a modal like *can*, we form the negative by putting *not* after the auxiliary verb:

He **is** *leaving.*   *He* **is not (isn't)** *leaving.*
He **can** *leave.*   *He* **cannot (can't)** *leave.*

With all other verbs we use *do not (don't)* and *does not (doesn't)* after the subject in the simple present, and *did not (didn't)* after the subject in the simple past. The verb is always a bare infinitive:

We **turn** *left.*   *We* **do not (don't) turn** *left.*
He **works** *well.*   *He* **does not (doesn't) work** *well.*
She **played** *well.*   *She* **did not (didn't) play** *well.*

12.3 Negative statements with 'never', etc.

We can make negative or near-negative statements with 'negative adverbs' like *never*, *hardly*, *hardly ever*, and *seldom*. *Never* is more emphatic than *not*. Compare: *I **don't drink** coffee. I **never drink** coffee.*

We can't use a negative adverb with a negative verb to make a 'double negative':

    *I **can hardly** keep awake.* (Not **I can't hardly**)
    Nobody phoned. (Not **Nobody didn't phone.**)

This is also true for *no*, *any* and their compounds:

*I**'ve got no** time.*	*I **haven't got any** time.*
*I**'ve seen no one.***	*I **haven't seen anyone**.*
*I **did nothing.***	*I **didn't do anything**.*
*I **went nowhere.***	*I **didn't go anywhere**.*

12.4 Negative questions: 'Can't you ...?'

We normally use short forms (*Can't*, etc.) to ask negative questions. Depending on stress and intonation, we can:

- express surprise:	***Don't you** know her?*
- persuade:	***Won't you** help me?*
- express annoyance:	***Can't you** be quiet?*
- make exclamations:	***Isn't it** hot in here!*

12.5 Tag questions

A tag question is a short question (e.g. *have you?/ haven't you?*) that follows a statement. Tag questions are:

- affirmative-negative: *You **like** fish, **don't** you?*
- negative-affirmative: *You **don't like** fish, **do** you?*

If our voice 'goes up', we are asking a real question which needs an answer:

    *You **locked** the door, **didn't** you? - Yes, I **did**.*

If our voice 'goes down', we are not really asking for information, but want the listener to agree that something is true:

    *You **locked** the door, **didn't** you?* (I assume so.)

12.6 Question-word questions

We ask question-word questions with: *Who(m), What, When, Which, Why, Where, Whose, How.*
The word order of question-word questions is:
question-word + auxiliary + subject:

statement:	*He is working.*
Yes/No question:	*Is he working?*
question-word:	***Why is he** working?*
	(Not **Why he is working?**)
statement:	*He arrives at 8.*
Yes/No question:	*Does he arrive at 8?*
question-word:	***When does he** arrive?*
	(Not **When he arrives?**)

12.7 'Who(m) ...?' as a question-word

Who(m) ...? is for people and asks for the object of a
sentence, usually a person's name or pronoun:
statement: *Frank met **Alice**.*
question: ***Who(m)** did Frank meet? - **Alice**.*
We often prefer *Who ...?* to *Whom ...?* in everyday
speech: ***Who** did you meet at the party?*

12.8 'What ...?' as a question-word

What ...? asks for a whole sentence:
What are you **doing**? - **I'm reading**.
or for the object of a sentence:
What are you **reading**? - **The paper**.
What can also combine with nouns:
What book(s) are you reading?
We also use *What* in a variety of combinations:
What time ...? What colour ...? What make ...?

12.9 'When ...?'/'Where ...?' as question-words

When ...? asks about time and we answer with adverbs
of time or prepositional phrases:
When is your flight? - **Tomorrow./At 4**.
Where ...? asks about place and we answer with whole
sentences, phrases or single words:
Where is he? **He's over there! Over there! There!**

12.10 'Which ...?' as a question-word

Which + noun asks about people or things:
> **Which child(ren)** *did you invite to the party?*
> **Which book(s)** *are you reading?*

Which refers to a limited choice:
> **Which** *do you prefer? - The red one.*

12.11 'Whose ...?' as a question word

Whose ...? asks about possession. The possessor is always a person and we expect the answer to be a name + 's, *(Kate's)* or a possessive *(mine*, etc.):
> **Whose coffee** *is this? - It's **Kate's**./**Mine***.

We can also say:
> **Whose is this** *coffee? - It's **Kate's**./**Mine***.

12.12 'Why ...?' as a question-word

Why ...? asks for a reason and we answer with a sentence beginning with *Because* or a *to-*infinitive:
> **Why** *are you running? - **To catch** the bus.*

12.13 'How ...?' as a question-word

We use *How ...?* basically to ask about manner:
> **How** *did you open it? - **With a pair of scissors**.*

We also use *How ...?* in different combinations:
> *How much?* (quantity): **How much bread** *is there?*
> *How much?* (price): **How much** *is it? - £20.*
> *How many?* (quantity): **How many eggs** *are there?*
> *How long?* (length): **How long** *is that skirt?*
> *How long?* (time): **How long** *did you wait?*

12.14 Subject-questions

A subject-question asks for the identity of the subject. There is no inversion and the question has the same word order as a statement:
> **statement**: **Someone** *paid*   *the waiter.*
> **question**: **Who**   *paid*   *the waiter? - **I did**.*

Answers generally need an auxiliary verb:
> **Who can** *play the piano? - **I can**.*
> **Who wants** *a lift? - **I do**.*

13 Conditional sentences

13.1 Conditions

A condition is something that has to be fulfilled before something else can happen. *If*, normally meaning 'on the condition that', is sometimes followed by *then*. If *then* is not stated, it is implied:

*If the rain stops, **(then)** we'll go for a walk.*

13.2 Type 1 conditionals: basic use and form

We use Type 1 conditionals to describe what (probably) will or won't happen. We form them by using present tenses after *if*, followed by *will*:

*If **she finishes** work early, **she will go** home.*
*If **she has finished** work by 4, **she will go** home.*

13.3 Type 1 conditionals: variations

There are three variations on this basic form:
1 'If' + present + modal (*may, might,* etc.)
We may use modals other than *will* in the main clause to show degrees of certainty [> 10.3, 10.8-9]:

*If it's fine today, **we may/must go** for a swim.*

2 'If + should' instead of 'if + present'
We use this form when we are doubtful or want to be very polite:

*If I **should** see him, **I'll ask** him to ring you.*

3 Imperative + 'and/or' + clause
We use this form for threats, requests, comments:

***Fool** around like that **and you'll fall off**!*

13.4 Type 2 conditionals: basic use and form

We use Type 2 conditionals:
1 to describe something that is reasonably possible:

*If you **went** by train, you **would get** there earlier.*

2 to describe what is totally impossible:

*If you **had** longer legs, you **would run** faster.*

We form Type 2 conditionals with *if* + past (or *if* + *could*) followed by *would*:

*If you **could run** faster, **you'd be** in the team.*

13.5 Type 2 conditionals: variations
There are two variations on this basic form:
1 'If + were' instead of 'if + past'
We use *were* rather than *was* in all persons after *if* to
express doubt or to sound formal:
> **If I were** in charge, **I'd make** some changes.
2 'If' + past + modal (*might, could*, etc.)
We may use modals other than *would* in the main
clause to show degrees of certainty:
> If **he knew** the facts, he **might tell** us what to do.

13.6 Type 3 conditionals: basic use and form
We often use Type 3 conditionals to express regret or
relief about things that can now never happen. We form
them with *if* + past perfect (or *if* + *could have*) followed
by *would have*:
> If **we'd gone** by car, we **would have saved** time.
> If **I could have stopped**, I **wouldn't have crashed**.

There is no 'special form' of *be* in Type 3:
> If **I had been** you, **I'd have accepted** the money.

13.7 Type 3 conditionals: variation
'If' + past perfect + modal (*might, could*, etc.)
We may use modals other than *would* in the main
clause to show degrees of certainty:
> If **he had known** the facts, **he might have told** us
> what to do.

13.8 'If not' and 'unless'
We can sometimes use *unless* in place of *if ... not* when
we mean 'except if'. *Unless* is stronger than *if not* and
we sometimes use it in 'threats'. We often use *unless*
with an affirmative verb:
> **If you don't pay**, they'll cut off the electricity.
> **Unless you pay**, they'll cut off the electricity.
We can't use *unless* in place of *if not* when *if not*
doesn't mean 'except if':
> I'll be amazed **if he doesn't** win. (= in the event that)

14 Direct and indirect speech

14.1 Direct speech

We use the term direct speech to describe the way we represent the spoken word in writing. We put quotation marks (also called 'inverted commas') outside all other punctuation marks, such as commas (,), full stops (.), question marks (?) and exclamation marks (!). They may be single ('...') or double ("..."). We put them at the beginning and end of each quotation, high above the base-line. We don't use dashes (-) or chevrons (<...>) to punctuate direct speech. We use only one question mark or exclamation mark to close direct speech:

'The shops close at 7 tonight,' John said.
'What time do the shops close?' Ann asked.
'Shut the window!' he cried.

14.2 Reporting verbs: 'say', 'tell' and 'ask' [> App 27]

We introduce direct and indirect speech with 'reporting verbs'. The commonest are *say, tell* and *ask*. We must always use a personal indirect object after *tell (tell somebody)*:

*He **told me** he was tired.* (Not *told to me*)

We can use *to me*, etc. after *say*, but we can't say *He said me*:

*'We must hurry,' **he said (to me)/he told me**.*

We can use *me*, etc. after *ask*, if we want to:

*She **asked (me)** if I was in a hurry.*

14.3 Indirect speech in the present

We use 'indirect speech' (sometimes called 'reported speech') when we are telling someone what another person said. We often use the same tenses as in the original when we report words that have just been spoken. Someone says 'I'm pleased' and we report it as: *He says/He said **he's pleased**.* Someone says 'I found it' and we report it as *She says/She said **she found it**.*

14.4 Indirect statements with tense changes

We tend to use past tenses in indirect speech because we are reporting past events, so we use the past tense of reporting verbs: *He **said** (that) ... He **told me** (that) ...* . When we report in the past, we generally move the reported clauses 'one tense back'. A useful general rule is: 'present becomes past and past becomes past perfect':

'I need a holiday,' Mac said.
  *Mac **said (that) he needed** a holiday.*
'I'm not wasting my time,' Sue said.
  *Sue **said (that) she wasn't wasting** her time.*
'I've been sleeping badly,' Wendy said.
  *Wendy **said (that) she'd been** sleeping badly.*
'I came by bus,' Tim said.
  *Tim **said (that) he came/had come** by bus.*
(The tense depends on the speaker's viewpoint.)
'I can speak French,' Joe said.
  *Joe **said (that) he could** speak French.*

14.5 Indirect questions

We don't use quotation marks or question marks in indirect questions. Question word-order changes back to statement word-order and we often move the reported question 'one tense back'.

We use *if* or *whether* after *ask* when we are reporting Yes/No questions [> 12.1]:
'Are you ready?' Jim asked.
  *Jim **asked (me) if/whether I was** ready.*

We use statement word order after question-words:
'How was Ann?' Tom asked. [> 12.6-13]
  *Tom asked (me) **how Ann was**.*

We keep the same word order when reporting subject-questions [> 12.14]:
'Who paid the waiter?' John asked.
  *John asked **who (had) paid** the waiter.*

14.6 Reporting the imperative

We report the imperative with suitable verbs + *to*-infinitive. The verb matches the function of the imperative (asking, telling, advising, etc.):

'Remember to post the letter,' she asked me.

She reminded me to post the letter.

When we report a negative imperative, we put *not* or *never* before the *to*-infinitive:

'Don't wait,' he said.

He asked/told me **not to wait**. (Not *to not*)

14.7 Reporting offers and suggestions

We can report offers and suggestions with *Shall I ...?* and *Should I ...?* in two ways:

'Shall/Should I phone her?' he asked me.

He wanted to know **if/whether he should phone** her.

He wanted to know **whether to phone** her. (Not *if to*)

14.8 Reporting requests for advice

We report requests for advice with question-words (*How shall/should I ...?*, etc.) in two ways:

'How shall/should I repair it?' he asked.

He wanted to know **how he should repair** it.

He wanted to know **how to repair** it.

We can use a *to*-infinitive after all question-words except *why*:

He wanted to know **why he should wait**.

14.9 When we use indirect speech

Indirect speech takes two forms: oral reporting (other people's instructions, conversations, etc.) and written reporting (newspaper reports, etc.). Here is an example of informal spoken reporting:

The boss wants you to go to the airport to pick up the company's guests. She says you're to take the company car. Oh, - and she asked me to tell you to phone if there are any flight delays.

15 The infinitive and the *-ing* form

15.1 The infinitive and the *-ing* form

We use a bare infinitive *(go)*, a *to*-infinitive *(to go)* or the *-ing* form *(going)* after many verbs and adjectives and some nouns. Sometimes only one form is grammatically correct, e.g. *let me **go**, fail **to do**, enjoy **doing***; sometimes more than one form is possible, e.g. *continue **to speak**, continue **speaking***.

15.2 The bare infinitive after verbs

We use the bare infinitive after the following:
- all modal verbs: *I **can't see** it.*
- *Let's* (suggestions):   ***Let's take** a taxi.*
- *let* (= allow):   *I won't **let you go**.*
- *make* (= compel):   *They **made us work** hard.*
- *would rather*:   *I'd **rather be** told the truth.*
- *had better*:   *You'd **better not tell** anyone.*

After *help*, we can use a bare infinitive, or a *to*-infinitive (slightly more formal):

    *Mother **helped me (to) do** my homework.*

15.3 The bare infinitive or the *-ing* form?

We use a noun or pronoun object + the bare infinitive or *-ing* after 'verbs of perception' like *feel, hear, listen to, look at, see, smell* and *watch*.

The bare infinitive refers to the complete action:

    *I **saw her reverse** the car out of the garage.*
    (i.e. I saw the whole action from start to finish.)
    *I **saw her reversing** the car out of the garage.*
    (i.e I saw part of the action.)

15.4 The *to*-infinitive to express purpose

To, so as to and *in order to* can express purpose:

    *I came here **to/in order to/so as to learn** English.*

We use *not to* for alternatives:

    *I came here **to learn** English, **not to waste** time.*

So as/in order not to express 'negative purpose':

    *Shut the door quietly **so as not to wake** the baby.*

15.5 Verb + *to*-infinitive [> App 28]

These verbs are followed only by a *to*-infinitive: *can('t) afford, fail, hurry, manage, offer, refuse*:
> He **can't afford to buy** a car. (Not **buying**)

15.6 Verb (+ object) + *to*-infinitive [> App 28]

These verbs can have a noun or pronoun object before the *to*-infinitive: *ask, beg, choose, expect, hate, help, like, love, need, prefer, want, wish*:
> I **want to speak** to the manager.
> (= I will speak to the manager.)
> I **want you to speak** to the manager.
> (= You will speak to the manager.)

15.7 Verb + object + *to*-infinitive

In the active, these verbs must always have an object before the *to*-infinitive: *advise, allow, forbid, invite, order, remind, teach, tell, warn*:
> My bank manager **advised me to repay** my loan.

15.8 Verb + *to*-infinitive or *that*

We can use a *to*-infinitive or *that* after these verbs: *agree, arrange, decide, expect, hope, promise*:
> I **agreed to accept** their offer.
> I **agreed that I would accept** their offer.

15.9 Adjective + *to*-infinitive [> App 25]

We use a personal subject (e.g. *he*) or we use *it* with adjectives like *clever, foolish, good, polite*:
> **He was kind** (enough) **to help** us.
> **It was kind** (of him) **to help** us.

We use only a personal subject with adjectives like *afraid, anxious, ashamed, eager, glad, keen, sorry*:
> **John is eager to please**. (Not **It is eager**)

Too before an adjective means 'excessively':
> He is **too weak to lift** it. (= not strong enough to)

Adjective + *enough* = 'to the necessary degree':
> He's **strong enough to lift** it. (= not too weak to)

15.10 The -ing form

We use the -ing form in three ways:

1 as a verb, when it is called a 'participle':

   He is **playing**. She is **writing**.

   Walking in the park yesterday, I heard a cuckoo.

   (= I was walking and I heard ...)

2 as an adjective [> 5.6]:

   I need some **boiling** water.

3 as a noun, called a 'gerund':

   I like **swimming**. (= the act of swimming)

15.11 The gerund

We can use the gerund in a number of ways, e.g.:

- as an uncountable noun in general statements:

   Dancing is fun.

- as an uncountable noun with *some, a lot of*, etc.:

   He went out to do **some shopping**.

- as an uncountable noun after prepositions:

   I disapprove **of boxing**.

- as a countable noun:

   That **painting** is by Bridget Riley.

- after 'No' in prohibitions:

   No Parking. No Smoking. No Waiting.

15.12 Verb + the -ing form

These verbs are followed only by the -ing form: *avoid, delay, deny, enjoy, fancy, finish, imagine, keep, mind, miss, prevent, risk, stop, suggest*:

   I **deny/denied taking** it. (Not *deny to take*)

We use -ing after *come* and *go* to refer to outdoor activities like *climbing, driving, riding, shopping*:

   Let's **go sailing**.

   Come shopping with us.

We use -ing or object + -ing after e.g. *stop*:

   You can't **stop him working**. (Not *his*)

We use a possessive + -ing after e.g. *delay*:

   Nothing will **delay our leaving**. (Not *us*)

Possessive or object + -ing after e.g. *imagine*:

   Imagine him/his saying such a thing!

15.13 Adjective + -*ing* or *to*-infinitive [> App 25]

We can use -*ing* or a *to*-infinitive after a great many adjectives and some nouns:

> **To lie/Lying** in the sun is **bad for you**.
> **It's bad for you** to **lie/lying** in the sun.

15.14 Adjective + -*ing* (participle) [> App 25]

We use only -*ing* after *busy, bored, occupied, tired*:

> I am **busy**. + I am **working**.   I'm **busy working**.

15.15 Common expressions + -*ing*

We use -*ing* after *it's no good, it's (not) worth, there's no point, what's the use of*:

> **It's no use crying** over spilt milk.

15.16 Preposition + -*ing* [> App 26]

We use -*ing*, not *to*, after prepositions:

> He left **without paying**. (Not *without to pay*)
> You'll get better **by practising**.
> I'm **sorry for complaining**. (adjective + preposition)
> I **apologize for interrupting**. (verb + preposition)

15.17 Verb + *to*-infinitive or -*ing*

After *begin, cease, continue* and *start* we can use *to* or -*ing* without any change in meaning:

> When did he **begin to speak/begin speaking**?

After *hate, like, love* and *prefer* there may be a slight change in meaning. Generally -*ing* refers to a situation in general and *to* refers to a future event:

> I **hate disturbing** you. (i.e. in general)
> I **hate to disturb** you. (e.g. but I'm about to)

15.18 Verb + *to* or -*ing*: different meanings

> **Remember to post** my letter. (future)
> I **remember posting** your letter. (past)
> I **regret to say** that I can't stay. (now)
> I **regret saying** what I said. (past)
> **Try to understand**. (= make the effort)
> **Try holding** your breath. (= experiment)

16 The sentence

Sentence word order

16.1 What is a sentence?

A sentence is a complete unit of meaning. It can take
one of the following forms:
- a **statement**: *The shops close/don't close at 7.*
- a **question**: *Do the shops close at 7?*
- a **command**: *Shut the door!*
- an **exclamation**: *What a slow train this is!*

A written sentence must begin with a capital letter and
end with a full stop (.), a question mark (?) or an
exclamation mark (!). It normally contains a finite verb,
that is a verb with a subject and tense:

He (subject) *has finished* (tense).

16.2 Basic word order

English is a word order language. The meaning of what
we say depends on the word order:

The dog bit the man.
The man bit the dog.

The basic word order is:

Subject	Verb	Object	Manner	Place	Time
Monica	*shouted at*	*me*	*angrily.*		
John	*has gone*			*home.*	
I	*watched*	*a film*			*last night.*

We can also begin with *time*:

Last night *I watched a film.*

Normally, we don't separate a subject from its verb and
a verb from its object. But there are a few variations on
the basic word order, for example:
- questions: **Did you take** *your car in for a service?*
- adverbs of frequency: *John* **never** *answers letters.*
- *-ly* adverbs: **Suddenly**, *the whole building shook.*
- conditionals: **Should you write**, *give her my love.*

50

The simple sentence

16.3 The simple sentence

The smallest sentence unit is the simple sentence. A simple sentence has one clause and finite verb:

> *I've eaten.*
> *John missed the train this morning.*

16.4 Five simple sentence patterns [> App 29]

1 subject + verb:
   My head   aches.
   Some verbs, such as *ache*, don't take an object.

2 subject + *be* + complement:
   Kerry   is   clever/an architect.
   We use an adjective or noun after the verb *be*.

3 subject + verb + direct object:
   My sister   enjoyed   the party.
   This is the most common type of sentence.

4 subject + verb + indirect object + direct object:
   They   gave Sam   a pen.
   *They **gave** a pen **to** Sam.* (Not **gave to Sam**)
   Other verbs like *give*, combining with *to*, are:
   lend, offer, pass, pay, sell, send, take, write.

   But note: *He **explained the situation to me**.*
   (Not **He explained me the situation.**)
   Similarly: *announce, describe, introduce.*

   They bought Sam a pen.
   *They **bought** a pen **for** Sam.* (Not **bought for Sam**)
   Other verbs like *buy*, combining with *for*, are:
   choose, cook, do, fetch, get, keep, order, save.

5 subject + verb + object + complement:
   They   made Sam   chairman.
   Similarly: *appoint, call, label, name, vote.*

The compound sentence

16.5 What is a compound sentence?

A compound sentence is two or more simple sentences joined together with co-ordinating conjunctions like *and, but, either ... or, neither ... nor*. All the clauses in a compound sentence are of equal importance and can stand on their own. When the subject is the same in all parts of the sentence, we don't usually repeat it:

*We fished all day, **but** (we) didn't catch a thing.*

Typical compound sentences are:

*I washed the car **and polished** it.*
*I **not only washed** it, **but polished** it **as well**.*
*You **either know** the answer **or** you **don't**.*
*He **neither speaks** French, **nor understands** it.*

We repeat the subject after *so* and *for* (= because):

*He couldn't find his pen, **so he wrote** in pencil.*
*I didn't call before, **for I thought** you'd be busy.*

The complex sentence

16.6 What is a complex sentence?

A complex sentence contains a main clause and one or more subordinate elements. If removed from a sentence, a main clause can often stand on its own. We form complex sentences in two ways:

1 by joining subordinate clauses to the main clause with conjunctions, for example, *as soon as*:
   The alarm was raised (main clause) **as soon as** *the fire was discovered.* (subordinate clause)

2 by using a *to*-infinitive or participle:
   ***To get** into university you have to pass a number of examinations.* (= If you want to get into ...)
   ***Seeing** the door open, the stranger entered the house.* (= When he saw the door open ...)

16.7 Types of complex sentence

16.7.1 Noun clauses (with *that* or *whether*)
*I'm afraid **(that) we've sold out of tickets**.*
*I don't know **whether you've heard the news**.*

16.7.2 Relative clauses (with *who(m), which, that*)
- ***who*** or ***that*** for people (subject):
  *He's the man **who/that lives** next door.*
- ***which*** or ***that*** for things/animals (subject):
  *This is the photo **which/that shows** my family.*
- ***who(m)*** or ***that*** for people (object):
  *She's the woman **who(m)/that** I met on holiday.*
  She's the woman I met on holiday.
- ***which*** or ***that*** for things/animals (object):
  *This is the photo **which/that I took**.*
  This is the photo I took.
  This is the box I keep my scissors in.
- ***whose*** (mainly for people):
  *She is the person **whose car** was stolen.*

16.7.3 Adverbial clauses [> App 30]
- of **time** with *when, after, as, as soon as*, etc:
  *I felt rested **when I got up this morning**.*
- of **place** with *where, wherever, anywhere*:
  *She visited the place **where she was born**.*
- of **manner** with *as, in the way that, as if*:
  *He looks **as if he's pleased**.*
- of **reason** with *because, as* or *since*:
  *We want a meal now **because we're hungry**.*
- of **concession** with *though, although, even if*:
  ***Though she's old**, she still goes out a lot.*
- of **purpose** with *so that, in order that, in case*:
  *We arrived early **so that we could get tickets**.*
  *Get there early **in case they sell out of tickets**.*
- of **result** with *so* + adjective/adverb + *(that)*:
  *He's **so annoyed (that) you can't speak to him**.*
- of **comparison** with *as, than, the ... the*:
  *I think she's more confident **than her brother is**.*

16.7.4 Present participle constructions

The present participle is the -*ing* form of a verb which we can use to join simple sentences:

*I **took care** to dial correctly. I tried again.*
***Taking care** to dial correctly, I tried again.*

We can use participle constructions in place of:
- compound sentences: *and recalled   recalling*:
  *She lay awake, **recalling** the events of the day.*
- relative clauses: *which is arriving   arriving*:
  *The train **arriving** on Platform 7 is from Rugby.*
- adverbial clauses of time, reason, etc.:
  ***Finding** the door open, I became suspicious.*
- in place of e.g. *she is*:
  ***She's** so excited, she'll never get to sleep.*
  ***Being** so excited, she'll never get to sleep.*

A participle must refer to the subject of both verbs:
***Watching** TV, I fell asleep.*
I was watching TV and I fell asleep.
(Not **Watching TV, the phone rang.**)
(The phone wasn't watching TV.)

16.7.5 Perfect participle constructions

We form these with *having* + past participle to describe something that has previously happened:
***Having made up** my mind, I felt better.*

16.7.6 Past participle constructions

We form these with the past participle of a verb. They are formal and we often use them in writing in place of the passive:
***When it is seen** from a distance, it looks smaller.*
***When seen** from a distance, it looks smaller.*
Or: ***Seen** from a distance, it looks smaller.*

We use past participle constructions in place of:
- relative clauses: *which is used   used*:
  ***The system used** in our school is very effective.*
- adverbial clauses of time, reason, etc.:
  ***Though delayed** in the post, your card's arrived.*

Summary: Fifteen basic grammar rules

1   English nouns don't have grammatical gender

- We use *he* or *she* for people and *it* for everything else:
  My accountant *says* **he** *is moving* **his** *office.*
  My doctor *says* **she** *is pleased with my progress.*
  I haven't been to the **exhibition**, *but I've read about* **it***.*
- *a/an*, *the* and adjectives don't have to 'agree' with nouns:
  a nice man, a nice woman, a nice book
  the old man, the old woman, the old book
  the old men, the old women, the old books

2   We use 's or s' (possession) mainly for people

We have to say:
  It's my **aunt's pen***.* (Not **It's the pen of my aunt.**)
If we want to show 'possession by things' we use a compound noun where possible:
  Where's my **car key***?* (rather than *the key of my car*)

3   Countable and uncountable nouns govern the use of articles

- We use *a/an* only in front of singular countable nouns:
  He's/She's **a teacher***.* (Not **He's/She's teacher.**)
  It's **an encyclopaedia***.* (Not **It's encyclopaedia.**)
  I want **some water** *please.* (Not **I want a water please.**)
- We use no article + plural/uncountable in general statements:
  (-) **Beans** *contain a lot of fibre.*
  (-) **Life** *is short;* (-) **Art** *is long.*

4   Countable and uncountable nouns govern the use of quantifiers

- We use *some/any/a lot of* with plural countable nouns *(apples)* and with uncountable nouns *(bread).*
- We use *some* in the affirmative: *There's* **some milk** *in the fridge.*
  and *any* in questions/negatives: *Is there* **any milk***?/There* **isn't any***.*
- We use *(a) few* and *(not) many* only with plural countable nouns:
  There are **a few complaints***. There* **aren't many complaints***.*
- We use *(a) little* and *(not) much* only with uncountable nouns:
  There is **a little bread***. There* **isn't much bread***.*
- We use *a lot of* in place of *much/many* in the affirmative:
  There are **a lot of complaints***. There's* **a lot of bread***.*
  (Not **There are many complaints.* *There's much bread.**)

5   The plural of 'a/an' is either no article or 'some/any'

- We use no article + plural noun when classifying/identifying:
     *It's **a peach**.   They're (-) **peaches**.*
- We use *any* or *some* to refer to quantity:
     *Do you want **a peach**?   Do you want **any peaches**?*
     *I want **a peach**.   I want **some peaches**.*

6   We don't use adjectives as nouns

- We can't use an adjective as if it were a noun:
     *He's **young**. He's **a young man**.* (Not **He's a young.**)
     *They're **young**. They're **young men**.*
     (Not **They're youngs.**)
Or we have to use words like *thing(s)* or *one(s)* which stand in place of nouns:
     *You **poor thing**!* (Not **You poor!* *)
     *I prefer **the red ones**.* (Not **I prefer the reds.**)
- We often use *the* + adjective to refer to the group as a whole:
     *This style appeals to **the young**.* (Not *the youngs*)
- We prefer the adjectival forms of nationality words to the noun forms:
     *He's/She's **Japanese**.* (rather than *a Japanese*)
     *He's/She's **English**.* (Not *an English*)
- Compound nouns are made up from noun + noun. In
     *I bought a **cotton blouse**.*
cotton is a noun which describes the noun that follows it (= a *blouse* made of *cotton*). It's not an adjective.

7   We use different prepositions for direction and position

- *to* (direction) contrasts with *at* or *in* (position):
     *She's gone **to school**. Now she's **at school**.*
     *She's gone **to bed**. Now she's **in bed**.*
- *into* (direction) contrasts with *in* (position):
     *He went **into the cinema**. Now he's **in the cinema**.*
- After *be* some nouns take only *in* and some take only *at*:
     *She's **in Europe**.* (Not **to Europe/at Europe**)
     *He's **at a party**.* (Not **to a party/in a party**)
- Some nouns take *at* or *in* depending on how we view them:
     *I'll meet you **at the airport**.* (= a meeting point)
     *I'll meet you **in the airport**.* (= inside the building)

8   We use different prepositions to refer to time

- *at*: exact time: *at 10 o'clock*; meal times: *at lunch time*; points of time: *at night*; festival-time: *at New Year*.
- *on*: days of the week: *on Monday*; parts of the day: *on Monday morning*; dates: *on June 1st*.
- *in*: parts of the day: *in the evening*; months: *in May*; years: *in 2050*; seasons: *in spring*; centuries: *in the 20th century*.

9   We use phrasal verbs where possible

*Don't **stand for** it.* (rather than *tolerate*)
***Take off** your hat./**Take** your hat **off**.* (rather than *Remove*)
Come in! (rather than *Enter!*)

10   Simple and progressive verb forms are used in different ways

- Most verbs have simple and progressive forms:
*I often **listen** to records.* (simple use: habit)
*I'm **listening** to a record.* (progressive: action going on now)
- Some verbs have different simple and progressive meanings:
*I **think** we should go by bus.* (= that's my opinion)
*Don't talk to me now. I'm **thinking**.* (= using my brain)
- Some verbs can never be used in the progressive because they describe states, not deliberate actions:
*She **loves** her children.* (Not **is loving**)

11   Modal verbs differ from ordinary verbs

Verbs like *can*, *must*, etc.:
- take a bare infinitive, not the infinitive with *to*:
*I **can see** you tomorrow.* (Not **can to see**)
- have no *-(e)s* in the 3rd person singular:
*The boss **can** see you now.* (Not **cans**)
They have two main uses:
1   In their first use, they express ideas like ability, necessity and permission and refer to present or future:
*I **must go now**. I **must go back tomorrow**.* (necessity)
We have to use a different verb to refer to the past:
*I **had to go** to the bank **yesterday**.* (Not **must go**)
2   In their second use, all of them except *shall* express varying degrees of certainty and have only two forms:
- present: *He **must be** right.*
- perfect or past: *He **must have been** right.*

12 **We use 'do', 'does' and 'did' to form questions and negatives in the simple present and simple past of ordinary verbs**

> ***Do you know*** *Tom?* (Not **Know you Tom?**)
> ***Does he know*** *Tom?* (Not **Knows he Tom?**)
> ***Did he meet*** *Tom?* (Not **Met he Tom?**)
> ***I don't know*** *Tom.* (Not **I not know Tom.**)
> ***He doesn't know*** *Tom.* (Not **He not know Tom.**)
> ***He didn't meet*** *Tom.* (Not **He not met Tom.**)
> ***When do you leave***? (Not **When you leave?**)
> ***When does he leave***? (Not **When he leaves?**)
> ***When did he leave***? (Not **When he left?**)

13 **We use only one negative word in a clause**

Words like *hardly* and *seldom* are negative, as well as *not*:
> *I* **can hardly** *keep awake.* (Not **I can't hardly keep**)
> *I've seen* **no one**. (Not **I haven't seen no one.**)

14 **We have to know which structure to use after a verb**

After some verbs we use:
- a bare infinitive: **Let** *me* **go**. (Not **Let me to go.**)
- a *to*-infinitive: *I* **want to go**. (Not **I want go.**)
- an -*ing* form: *I* **enjoy working**. (Not **I enjoy to work.**)
- *to* or -*ing*: *He* **continued to speak**. *He* **continued speaking**.

We can use various structures after verbs like *suggest*:
> *I* **suggest** *(that)* **you write** *to him.* (Not **suggest to write**)
> *I* **suggest** *(that)* **you should write** *to him.*
> *I* **suggest writing** *to him.* (Not **suggest to write**)

15 **English is a word order language**

- (Time) | Subject | Verb | Object | Manner | Place | (Time):
> *I speak English well.* (Not **I speak well English.**)
- We don't separate a subject from its verb:
> **They went** *to Paris.* (Not **They to Paris went.**)
- We don't separate a verb from its object:
> *He* **banged his hand** *on the table.* (Not **He banged on the table his hand.**)
- Every English sentence must have a subject:
> **It's hot** *today.* (Not **Is hot today.**)
- Verbs such as *like*, *want* and *have* always take an object:
> *Do you like this coffee? - Yes, I* **like it**. (Not **Yes, I like.**)

58

APPENDIX 1 [> 1.2]
Some common noun endings
1.1 People who do things
-**ant**: *assistant*; -**ar**: *beggar*; -**eer**: *engineer*; -**er**: *driver*; -**ian**: *historian*; -**ist**: *pianist*; -**or**: *actor*.

1.2 People who come from places
-**an**: *Roman*; -**er**: *Londoner*; -**ese**: *Milanese*; -**ian**: *Athenian*; -**ite**: *Muscovite*.

1.3 Nouns from verbs
-**age**: *postage*; -**al**: *arrival*; -**ance**: *acceptance*; -**ence**: *existence*; -**ery**: *discovery*; -**ion**: *possession*; -**ment**: *agreement*; -**tion**: *attention*.

1.4 Nouns related to adjectives
-**ance**/-**ence**: *abundance*, *absence*; -**ancy**/-**ency**: *constancy*, *consistency*; -**ety**: *anxiety*; -**ity**: *activity*; -**ness**: *happiness*.

1.5 Nouns derived from other nouns
-**dom**: *kingdom*; -**ful**: *mouthful*; -**hood**: *boyhood*; -**ism**: *sexism*.

1.6 Endings meaning 'small'
-**en**: *kitten*; -**ette**: *maisonette*; -**ie**: *laddie*; -**let**: *booklet*.

APPENDIX 2 [> 1.4.1]
Nouns not normally countable in English
advice, bread, chess, clothing, damage, food, fruit, grass, hair, help, homework, housework, jewellery, laughter, thunder and lightning, linen, luggage, macaroni, meat, money, music, news, peel, rubbish, soap, steam, toast, traffic, travel, weather, work.

APPENDIX 3 [> 1.4.2]
Partitives
3.1 Amounts/quantities
a bar of chocolate/soap, a block of cement, a bunch of flowers, an item of news, a pack of cards, a loaf of bread, a slice of meat.

3.2 'Containers'
a bottle of milk, a box of matches, a can of beer, a pot of tea, a glass of water, a jug of water, a tin of biscuits, a vase of flowers.

3.3 Small quantities
a blade of grass, a breath of air, a crust of bread, a drop of rain, a grain of rice, a lock of hair, a pat of butter, a scrap of paper.

3.4 Measures
a gallon of petrol, a litre of oil, an ounce of gold, a pint of milk, a kilo of coffee, a metre of cloth.

3.5 A game of ...
baseball, billiards, cards, chess, football, table-tennis, tennis, volleyball.

3.6 Abstract
a bit of advice, a branch of knowledge, a piece of research, a spot of trouble.

3.7 Types/species
a brand of soap, a kind of biscuit, a species of insect, a type of drug, a variety of pasta.

3.8 A pair of ...
boots, braces, glasses, gloves, knickers, pants, pliers, pyjamas, scissors, shoes, shorts, skates, skis, slippers, socks, stockings, tights, trousers.

Appendix 4 [> 5.2]
Common adjectival forms
4.1 Suffixes
-able (capable of being): *changeable*; **-ible** (like *-able*): *possible*; **-ful** (full of, having): *beautiful*; **-ful/-less**: *careful - careless*; **-i(a)n** (historical period, etc.): *Victorian*; **-ish** (have the - sometimes bad - quality): *foolish*; (colour): *reddish*; **-ive** (capable of being): *attractive*; **-less** (without): *lifeless*; **-like** (resembling): *businesslike*; **-ly** (have this quality): *friendly*. Others: **-al**: *mechanical*; **-ant**: *hesitant*; **-ar**: *circular*; **-ary**: *visionary*; **-ate**: *affectionate*; **-ent**: *sufficient*; **-ic**: *energetic*; **-ic/ical**: *economic - economical*; **-ious**: *glorious*; **-ist**: *racist*; **-ory**: *sensory*; **-ous**: *humorous*.

4.2 Prefixes
anti-: *anti-war*; **dis-**: *dishonest*; **il-**: *illegal*; **im-**: *impossible*; **in-**: *indifferent*; **ir-**: *irrational*; **un-**: *unthinkable*. Others: **a-**: *amoral*; **over-**: *overdue*; **pre-**: *pre-war*; **super-**: *superhuman*; **under-**: *underdone*.

Appendix 5 [> 5.6]
Adjectives ending in *-ed /-ing*
alarmed, alarming; amazed, amazing; annoyed, annoying; confused, confusing; depressed, depressing; embarrassed, embarrassing; excited, exciting; exhausted, exhausting; frightened, frightening; horrified, horrifying; moved, moving; pleased, pleasing; relaxed, relaxing; satisfied, satisfying; shocked, shocking; surprised, surprising; terrified, terrifying; worried, worrying.

Appendix 6 [> 5.7]
'The' + adjective
the aged, the blind, the dead, the deaf, the disabled, the dumb, the elderly, the guilty, the handicapped, the healthy, the homeless, the innocent, the living, the mentally-ill, the middle-aged, the old, the poor, the rich, the sick, the unemployed, the young.

Appendix 7 [> 5.8]
Nationality adjectives and nouns
7.1 the + -ese or -ss
He's/She's **Japanese**.
I like **the Japanese**.
the Chinese, the Lebanese, the Maltese, the Portuguese, the Sudanese, the Taiwanese, the Swiss.

7.2 (the) + plural in -s
He's/She's **Italian**.
I like **(the) Italians**.
-ian: *(the) Argentinians, (the) Austrians, (the) Belgians, (the) Brazilians, (the) Egyptians, (the) Hungarians, (the) Russians.*
-an: *(the) Americans, (the) Mexicans, (the) Koreans, (the) Venezuelans.*
other -s endings: *(the) Cypriots, (the) Germans, (the) Greeks, (the) Kuwaitis, (the) Thais, (the) Turks.*

7.3 Two forms
He's/She's **Danish**.
I like **the Danish/the Danes**.
the Polish/the Poles, the Finnish/the Finns, the Spaniards/the Spanish, the Swedish/the Swedes.

7.4 the + -ch or -sh
He's/She's **Dutch**.
I like **the Dutch**.
the British, the English, the French, the Irish, the Welsh.

APPENDIX 8 [> 6.3]
Adverbs with and without -*ly*
8.1 Without + -*ly*
*The train went **fast**.*
better, big, early,
far, long, straight, well.

8.2 Two forms often used in the same way
*I bought it **cheap/cheaply**.*
clean/cleanly, clear/clearly,
close/closely, dear/dearly,
fair/fairly, fine/finely,
firm/firmly, first/firstly,
loud/loudly, quick/quickly,
quiet/quietly, slow/slowly.

8.3 Two forms used in different ways
*We worked **hard**.*
*We **hardly** worked at all.*
drink **deep/deeply** regret
go **direct**/I'll come **directly**
go **easy**/win **easily**
aim **high**/think **highly** of you
arrive **last/Lastly**, I think ...
arrive **late/Lately**, I've seen ...
go **near/nearly** finished
10 am **sharp**/speak **sharply**
stop **short**/see you **shortly**
open **wide**/it's **widely** known

APPENDIX 9 [> 6.6]
Adverbs of frequency
(arranged on a scale)
- always
- almost/nearly always
- generally, regularly, usually
- frequently, often
- sometimes, occasionally
- seldom, rarely
- almost never, hardly ever
- not ... ever, never

APPENDIX 10 [> 6.7]
Adverbs of degree
*I'm **barely/scarcely** ready*
*it's **a bit** expensive*
*the water's warm **enough***
*it's **fairly/rather** hot*
*I **quite** like it*
*it's **hardly** right*

APPENDIX 11 [> 6.8]
Intensifiers
11.1 Very
+ adjective: ***very** nice*
+ adverb: ***very** slowly*
+ -ed: ***very** interested*

11.2 Very much
+ comparative:
*I'm **very much** better.*
+ verb:
*I like it **very much**.*

11.3 -*ly* in place of 'very'
awfully sorry
extremely helpful
frightfully lazy
particularly interesting
really slowly
terribly confused

11.4 -*ly* in fixed phrases
badly needed
bitterly cold
deeply hurt
greatly appreciated
highly respected
painfully embarrassed
richly deserved
severely ill
thoroughly fed-up
totally idiotic

APPENDIX 12 [> 6.10]
Some viewpoint adverbs
actually
as a matter of fact
as a rule
basically
briefly
by and large
frankly
honestly
in my opinion
in principle
in short
naturally
obviously
on the whole
possibly
strictly speaking
surprisingly

APPENDIX 13 [> 7.1]
Prepositions
13.1 One-word prepositions
about 10 o'clock
above my room
across the street
after lunch
against the wall
along the river bank
among my friends
at the station
before breakfast
behind the curtain
sit *beside* me
between you and me
go *by* taxi
down the street
during the summer
this is *for* you
a present *from* me
in the building
inside the building
go *into* the kitchen
near the station
a piece *of* cake
on the shelf
jump *onto* the stage
opposite the station
over the moon
walk *past* the house
since yesterday
through this door
wait *till* tomorrow
went *to* London
under the bed
up the street
come *with* me
don't go *without* me

13.2 Two or more words
according to him
ahead of us
apart from that
as a result of this
because of you
by comparison with that
in case of fire
in front of the house
instead of you
sit *next to* me
on account of this
with regard to your letter

APPENDIX 14
To, at, in [> 7.2]
14.1 at or in + noun
They went to the airport.
They are at/in the airport.
At (= a meeting point)
In (= inside the building)
the cinema, the theatre, the zoo,
the car park, the garage, the
office; the bank, the library, the
post office, the restaurant; at/in
church (to pray); at/in the church
(for some other reason); at/in
school (to learn); at/in the school
(for some other reason); in
hospital (as a patient); at/in the
hospital (for some other reason).

14.2 to + noun/at + noun
They've gone to a concert.
They're at a concert.
events: a dinner, a funeral, a
meeting, a wedding.
public places: the station, the
library, the doctor's.
'attending': church, school. Note
that *home* is a special case:
They've gone home.
(Not *gone to home*)
She's at home.
(Not *to home*)
addresses: his sister's, 24 Cedar
Avenue.

14.3 to + noun/in + noun
They've gone to Europe.
They're in Europe.
large areas: Texas, the Andes,
the Antarctic, the Sahara, the
Mediterranean.
towns and parts of towns: New
York, Manhattan, Paris.
outside areas: the park, the
square, Oxford Street, the old
town, the mountains.
rooms: the bathroom, the
bedroom, the kitchen, the waiting
room, the lounge,
the bathroom, the lavatory.
nouns with no article: bed,
chapel, church, hospital.

Type 1 phrasal verbs:
Verb + preposition + object
(non-idiomatic)
Key: sby = somebody
       stg = something

advise against doing stg
agree about stg
agree to a proposal
agree with sby
apologize to sby for stg
apply to sby for stg
approve of sby/stg
arrive at/in
become of sby
begin with/by doing stg
believe in sby/stg
belong to sby/stg
borrow from sby
deal with sby/a problem
depend on sby/stg
differ from sby/stg
dream about/of (doing)
fail in e.g an exam
insist on (doing) stg
knock at (the door)
know of/about sby/stg
laugh at/about sby/stg
listen to sby/stg
look after sby/stg
look at sby/stg
look for sby/stg
object to sby/stg
pay for sby/stg
quarrel with sby about stg
read about sby/stg
refer to sby/stg
rely on sby/stg
reply to sby
report on sby/stg to sby
resign from a job
retire from one's job
search for sby/stg
succeed in (doing) stg
suffer from an illness
talk to sby about stg
taste of stg
trade with sby/in stg
vote for/against sby/stg
wait for sby/stg
wish for stg
write to sby/about stg

Type 1 phrasal verbs:
Verb + object + preposition +
object (non-idiomatic)
Key: sby = somebody
       stg = something

accuse sby of stg
adapt stg to stg
add stg to stg
admire sby for stg
advise sby about stg
appoint sby a/to a job
arrange stg for sby
associate sby/stg with
attach stg to stg
betray a secret to sby
blame sby for stg
charge stg to an account
charge sby with a crime
claim stg from sby
combine stg with stg
compare sby/stg with
compensate sby for stg
congratulate sby on stg
defend sby from stg
describe stg to sby
discuss stg with sby
divide a number by
excuse sby for stg
explain stg to sby
forgive sby for stg
hide stg from sby
include stg in stg else
inform sby of/about stg
insure sby against stg
interest sby in stg
invest money in stg
lend stg to sby
refer sby/stg to sby
remind sby of sby/stg
repeat stg to sby
reserve stg for sby
return stg to sby
rob sby of stg
search sby for stg
share stg with sby
steal stg from sby
stop sby from doing stg
tell sby about stg
translate stg from/into
turn stg into stg else
use stg for stg else

APPENDIX 17 [> 7.5.1]
Type 1 phrasal verbs:
Verb + preposition + object
(idiomatic)
eggs **don't agree with** me
(= have a bad effect)
you'll have to **answer to** him
(= explain yourself)
you're **asking for** trouble
(= inviting)
I didn't **bargain for** this
(= not prepared for)
please **call for** me at 6
(= come and collect)
can I **call on** you tomorrow?
(= visit)
I **came across** this old book
(= found)
what **came over** you?
(= affected)
I could **do with** a drink
(= want one)
I won't **fall for** that trick
(= be deceived by)
he's **fallen for** her
(= fallen in love with)
she **flew into** a rage
(= became very angry)
I **gather from** John that ...
(= understand)
stop **getting at** me
(= constantly criticizing)
she's **got over** her illness
(= recovered from)
you can't **get round** me
(= persuade)
let's **go after** him
(= try and catch)
the dog **went for** me
(= attacked)
I'll **go into** the matter
(= investigate)
the house **grew on** me
(= became attractive)
I must **hand it to** you
(= praise you)
he **headed for** home
(= went)
I won't **hear of** it
(= consider)
help him to some potatoes
(= serve him with)

I **hit on** this idea
(= had/got this idea)
keep at it
(= work persistently)
leave it to me
(= give me the responsibility)
he **lives on** fruit
(= that's what he eats)
we'll **look into** it
(= investigate it)
I can't **make** anything **of** it
(= understand)
I'll **press for** a pay rise
(= try hard for)
she's **reading for** a degree
(= studying)
she's **rolling in** money
(= has a lot of money)
will he **run for** president?
(= try to be elected)
a bus **ran into** my car
(= hit it)
he **ran through** a fortune
(= spent quickly)
don't **rush into** it
(i.e. without consideration)
see about fixing that fence
(= arrange)
I **saw through** it
(= was not deceived by)
I'll **sleep on** your suggestion
(= decide later)
I hope you'll **stand by** me
(= support)
I won't **stand for** it
(= tolerate)
we must **step on** it
(= hurry up)
I hope you'll **stick by** me
(= remain loyal)
he **takes after** his father
(= resembles)
work is **telling on** him
(= having a bad effect)
he **touched on** the subject
(= mentioned it)
I've been **turned off** it
(= made to lose interest)
I can't be **waiting on** you
(= serving you)
I **walked into** a trap
(i.e. carelessly)

Type 2 phrasal verbs:
Verb + particle + object
(non-idiomatic)
Key: sby = somebody
stg = something
Particles strengthen or
extend the effect of the verb.
When referring to *things*, we can
put the object after or before the
particle:
*He **knocked over a cup**.*
*He **knocked a cup over**.*
*He **knocked it over**.*
When referring to *people*, we
generally can't put the object after
the particle:
*He **knocked the boy over**.* (Not
over the boy*)
*He **knocked him over**.*

18.1 about/around
here and there:
carry sby/stg about/around
follow sby about/around

18.2 across
from one side to another:
allow sby across
push sby across

18.3 along
in a forward direction:
help sby along
pass stg along
strengthening the verb:
ask sby along
bring sby/stg along

18.4 away
distance:
carry sby/stg away
push sby/stg away
detachment:
cut stg away
pull stg away
disappearance:
sweep stg away
wipe stg away
tidying:
fold stg away
put stg away

18.5 back
returning:
ask sby back
give stg back
out of the way:
move sby/stg back
tie stg back
prevention:
hold sby/stg back
repetition:
play stg back
read stg back

18.6 down
downwards direction:
bring sby/stg down
throw stg down
destruction:
burn stg down
knock sby/stg down
secure firmly:
fix stg down
screw stg down
reduction:
boil (a liquid) down
let (tyres) down
completeness:
close (a shop) down
drink stg down
writing:
copy stg down
write stg down
prevent from rising:
hold sby/stg down
keep sby/stg down

18.7 in
outside to inside:
bring sby/stg in
give (homework) in
arrival/location:
book sby in
find sby in (e.g. at home)
confine:
fence stg in
keep sby/stg in
inclusion:
throw stg in
fit sby/stg in
inwards/destruction:
beat (a door) in
smash stg in

18.8 off
detachment/removal:
brush stg off
let sby off (a bus)
wipe stg off
distance:
beat (an animal/insects) off
frighten sby/an animal off
division/disconnection:
divide stg off
turn (the lights) off
completion:
finish stg off

18.9 on
attachment:
fit stg on
have stg on (= wear)
stick stg on
in a forward direction:
pass stg on
send stg on

18.10 out
inside to outside:
drive (a car) out
help sby out (of a car)
movement 'out':
call (a doctor) out
pay money out
pick sby/stg out (= choose)
exclusion/prevention:
fence (animals) out
leave stg out (= not include)
removal/disappearance:
cut (a picture) out
turn (the lights) out
extension:
hold (your hand) out
spread (a cloth) out
make audible or clear:
copy stg out
spell stg out
thoroughly:
check sby/stg out
sort sby/stg out
distribution:
give things out
share things out
to a conclusion:
talk stg out
think stg out

18.11 over
from one side to another:
carry sby/stg over
help sby over
with verbs of 'inviting':
ask sby over
bring sby/stg over
from end to end:
check stg over
wipe stg over
to the ground:
knock sby/stg over
push sby/stg over

18.12 round
circular:
drive (a car) round
enclosing:
fence (a garden) round
with verbs of 'inviting':
ask sby round
have sby round
distribution:
pass stg round
changing position:
move things round

18.13 through
from one side to another:
show sby through
thoroughly:
heat stg through
in two pieces:
slice stg through

18.14 up
upwards:
pull sby/stg up
from off a surface:
pick stg up
completely:
drink stg up
open stg up
into smaller pieces:
break stg up
cut stg up
out of bed:
get sby up
let sby up
confining:
button (a coat) up
lock sby/stg up

Type 2 phrasal verbs:
Verb + particle + object
(idiomatic)

they **blew** the bridge **up**
(= destroyed by explosion)
she's **brought up** four sons
(= reared, educated)
you can't **buy** me **off**
(= e.g. bribe me)
we'll **call off** the meeting
(= cancel)
who's **covering up** the facts?
(= concealing)
I've been **cut off**
(= disconnected on phone)
shall I **do** your room **out**?
(= clean it)
shall I **drop** you **off** here?
(= let you get out of the car)
please **fill in/out** this form
(= supply details)
let's **fix up** a date
(= make arrangements)
who **gave away** the secret?
(= revealed it)
who'll **give** the bride **away**?
(i.e. at the wedding)
I've **given up** smoking
(= stopped the habit)
you're **having** me **on**
(= deceiving me as a joke)
we were **held up** in the fog
(= delayed)
he's **keeping** us **on**
(= continuing to employ)
they've **laid off** 100 men
(= stopped employing)
I can't **lay out** more money
(= spend)
he **let** everyone **down**
(= disappointed)
please **let** the children **off**
(= don't punish)
who **let** the secret **out**?
(= revealed it)
please **look** the word **up**
(i.e. in the dictionary)
look me **up** when you're back
(= contact me)
I can just **make** him **out**
(= see him with difficulty)

you've **made** that story **up**
(= invented)
you **made** your face **up**
(= applied cosmetics)
they **missed** our names **out**
(= didn't include)
I've **packed** my job **in**
(= stopped)
I'll **pay** you **back** for this
(= get my revenge)
point the place **out** to me
(= show)
we've **pulled off** a deal
(= been successful)
can we **put** the meeting **off**?
(= postpone)
she's **put** her hip **out**
(= dislocated)
he always **runs** her **down**
(= criticizes unfairly)
he was **run over** by a car
(= knocked down)
you're **sending** me **up**
(= ridiculing by imitating)
who **set up** this scheme?
(= organized it)
I can't **shake** this cold **off**
(= get rid of it)
we'll **sort** this mess **out**
(= clear up)
I'll **spell** it **out** to you
(= make it absolutely clear)
we must **step up** production
(= increase)
we're **taking on** new staff
(= employing)
he's **taking** me **out** tonight
(e.g. for a meal)
he **told** us **off**
(= reprimanded)
top the battery **up**
(= fill it)
they're **turning** us **out**
(= making us leave)
can you **win** him **over**?
(= persuade him to agree)
they **wiped** the village **out**
(= destroyed)
we'll **work** this problem **out**
(= solve it)
my car was **written off**
(= made unrepairable)

APPENDIX 20 [> 7.5.3]
Type 3 phrasal verbs:
Verb + particle (no object)
(idiomatic)
he's **acting up**
(= behaving badly)
look who's **blown in**
(= arrived unexpectedly)
prices have **bottomed out**
(= are at their lowest level)
she **catches on** fast
(= learns fast)
cheer up!
(= be cheerful!)
prices have **come down**
(= been reduced)
my plan **came off**
(= succeeded)
my engine's **cut out**
(= stopped working)
let's **dress up**
(= put on special clothes)
Dad's just **dropped off**
(= fallen asleep)
we **fell about**
(= collapsed with laughter)
we've **fallen out**
(= quarrelled)
I told him to **go ahead**
(= take action)
they really **get on**
(= have a good relationship)
it's time you **got up**
(= rose from bed)
they'll never **give in**
(= surrender)
what's **going on**?
(= happening)
don't **hold back** now
(= hesitate)
it's hard to **keep on**
(= continue)
I can't **keep up**!
(= stay at your level)
I'm going to **knock off**
(= stop work)
please don't **let on**
(= reveal the secret)
I love to **lie in**
(= stay in bed late)
look out!
(= take care! i.e. danger)

things are **looking up**
(= improving)
he took it and **made off**
(= ran away)
stop **messing about**
(= acting carelessly)
mind out!
(= be careful! i.e. danger)
later, he **opened up**
(= talked more freely)
come on, **own up**
(= confess)
he **passed away** last year
(= died)
when I heard it, I **passed out**
(= fainted)
your scheme didn't **pay off**
(= succeed)
this car's **playing up**
(= giving trouble)
pull in here
(= stop just off the road)
he **pulled up** suddenly
(= used the brakes to stop)
I've got to **ring off**
(= end the phone call)
our supplies **ran out**
(= were used up)
we're **selling up**
(= selling all we have)
winter has **set in**
(= begun)
when do you **set out**?
(= begin your journey)
don't **show off**
(= try to be noticed)
shut up!
(informal/rude = be quiet!)
slow down!
(= go at a gentler pace!)
I've **switched off**
(= I'm not listening)
I'm going to **turn in**
(= go to bed)
don't **wait up** for me
(= delay going to bed)
who's going to **wash up**?
(= wash the dishes)
watch out!
(= be careful! i.e. danger)
how did your plan **work out**?
(= develop)

APPENDIX 21 [> 7.5.4]
Type 4 phrasal verbs:
Verb + particle + preposition (idiomatic)

it **boils down to** this
(= can be summarized as)
cash in on the price rise
(= take advantage of)
it all **comes down to** this
(= means this)
he's **come in for** criticism
(= received)
he **came up with** a good idea
(= produced)
face up to it
(= accept it honestly)
can you **fill** me **in on** it?
(= inform me)
he **got away with** it
(= escaped punishment for)
I'll **get on to** him
(= contact)
I can't **go through with** it
(= finish this difficult thing)
keep in with him
(= stay on good terms)
let me **in on** it
(= share information)
I can't **live up to** it
(= keep the high standard)
I **look forward to** it
(= expect to enjoy)
this won't **make up for** it
(= compensate for)
put in for a rise
(= make a formal request)
who **put** you **up to** this?
(= gave you the idea)
I won't **put up with** it
(= tolerate)
we've **run out of** rice
(= used all we had)
speak up for him
(= state your support)
I'll **stand in for** you
(= act in your place)
we'll **stick up for** you
(= support you)
don't **take it out** on me
(= punish me for it)
talk him **out of** it
(= persuade him not to do it)

APPENDIX 22 [> 8.3]
Some stative verbs
* = these have non-stative uses
22.1 Feelings (I like, etc.)
*admire, *appreciate, (it) astonish,
*(it) attract, believe in, care about,
dislike, esteem, *hate, *hope, *(it)
interest, *like, *love, *mean,
*mind, *regret, (can't) stand, trust,
*value.

22.2 Thinking (I know, etc.)
agree, *appreciate, believe,
*consider, disagree, disbelieve,
*expect, *feel, *find, *hear (= be
told), hear of (= know about),
*imagine (= think), know, *realize,
*recognize, *regard, *see (=
understand), *suppose, *think (=
believe), understand, *wonder.

22.3 Wants (I want, etc.)
desire, fancy, need, prefer,
require, want, wish.

22.4 The senses
*hear, notice, *observe, perceive,
*(can) see, *smell, *(can) taste.

22.5 'Being', 'having', etc.
add up (= make sense), (can)
afford, *appear (= seem), belong
(to), come about, (it) concern,
consist of, contain, *correspond
to/with, *cost, *count, *depend,
deserve, differ from, equal, *feel,
*fit, happen to, have/have got,
*hold (= contain), *(it) include,
keep + -ing, know sby, *look (=
appear), own, possess, (it) say,
seem, *(it) smell (of), *(it) sound
(= seem), *(it) stand for, (it) suit (=
be suitable), *(it) taste (of), *tend,
*weigh.

APPENDIX 23 [> 9.9]
'Have' + noun

Eating/drinking: *have breakfast, lunch, etc., a drink, a meal, a snack, a/some coffee, a sandwich.*

Rest/sleep: *have a rest, a sleep, a nap, a lie-down, a day off, a holiday, a dream, a nightmare.*

Washing, etc.: *have a bath, a perm, a wash, a shower, a shave, a haircut, a shampoo, a massage.*

Appointments and pastimes: *have an appointment, a date, an interview, a meeting, a lesson, a game, a break, a good time, fun, a nice day, a ride, a walk.*

Travel: *have a trip, a drive, a lift, a good journey, a good flight.*

The weather: *have some/a lot of rain, good/bad weather, fog, a lovely day.*

Illnesses, medical: *have a cold, a cough, a headache, a fever, a temperature, flu, measles, a pain, a baby, a breakdown.*

Personal qualities: *have a bad temper, (no) brains, an eye for, green fingers, guts, no conscience, sense, a sense of humour, a sweet tooth.*

Relationships, opportunities: *an advantage, an argument, a chat, a choice, difficulty, a discussion, an effect, a guess, influence, a nerve, no business, an opportunity, a problem, a reason, a row, a talk, the time.*

Emotional states, etc.: *have a feeling, an idea that, the faintest idea, a good laugh (about something), a lot to put up with, a mind to, an opinion, a plan, a point of view, second thoughts, a shock, a suggestion.*

APPENDIX 24 [> 9.13]
Common combinations with 'do' and 'make'
24.1 Combinations with 'do'

work, etc.: *do business, a deal (with), one's duty, a job, something for a living, a service, work.*

household tasks: *do the cooking, the housework, the ironing, the shopping, the washing, the washing-up.*

places: *do the city by night, the sights, Rome in a day.*

speed/distance: *do a hundred km an hour, thirty miles to the gallon.*

subjects, etc.: *do Art, French, an experiment, one's homework, a lesson, research.*

routine tasks: *do the beds, the flowers, the kitchen, one's hair, one's teeth.*

24.2 Combinations with 'make'

make an accusation, an agreement, an apology, an application, an attempt, a bargain, a bed, a (phone) call, a change, a choice, a claim, a comment, a contribution, a criticism, a decision, a deduction, a demand, a discovery, an effort (to), an error, an escape, an excuse, a fortune, a guess, a habit of something, history, an impression, an inquiry, a journey, a loss, a mess, a mistake, money, a move (= start to go), a name for oneself, a noise, an offer, a profit, progress, a promise, a proposal, a record, a reference, a remark, a report, a request, room (for), rules, sense (of), a start, a success of, a trip, trouble, use of, war, one's way to a place (= go there), a will.

APPENDIX 25 [> 15.9/13/14]
Adjective + to, that, -ing
I'm able to/unable to
I'm afraid to/that
I was angry to/that
I'm anxious to/that
I'm ashamed to/that
It's awful to/that/-ing
It's bad to/that/-ing
It's better/best to/that/-ing
I'm busy -ing
I'm/It's certain to/that
It's difficult to/-ing
I'm eager to/that ... should
I'm/It's easy to, It's easy -ing
It's essential to/that ... should
It's expensive to/-ing
It's foolish to/-ing
I'm glad to/that
It's no good -ing
It's great to/that/-ing
I'm happy to/that/-ing
I'm hopeful that
It's hopeless to/-ing
It's horrible to/that/-ing
It's important to/that ... should
I'm keen to/that ... should
I'm last to
It's lovely to/that/-ing
I'm/It's lucky to/that/-ing
It's nice to/that/-ing
I'm obliged to
It's pleasant to/that/-ing
I'm prepared to
I'm quick to/-ing
I'm ready to
I'm/It's right to
It's right that ... should
I'm/It's sad to/that/-ing
It's silly to/that/-ing
I'm slow to/-ing/It's slow -ing
I'm sorry to/that
It's strange to/that/-ing
It's stupid to/-ing
I'm sure to (= likely)
It's sure that (= certain)
It's true to (say)/that
It's vital to/that ... should
It's wise to/-ing
It's worth -ing
I'm/It's wrong to/-ing
It's wrong that ... should

APPENDIX 26 [> 15.16]
Adjective + preposition
Key: sby = somebody
       stg = something
absent from a place
afraid of sby/stg
angry at/about sby/stg
angry with sby
annoyed at/about stg
annoyed with sby
anxious about/over sby/stg
ashamed of sby/stg
aware of sby/stg
awful at (doing) stg
bad at (doing) stg
bored by/with sby/stg
busy at/with stg
certain of/about facts
clever at (doing) stg
content with stg
curious about sby/stg
different from/to sby/stg
eager for stg
excited about/at/by/over
faithful to sby/stg
famous for (doing) stg
fond of sby/stg
free from danger/of charge
full of stg
glad about stg
good at (doing) stg
grateful to sby for stg
happy about/at/over/with
interested in/by sby/stg
jealous of sby/stg
keen on (doing) stg
kind to sby
married to sby
nervous of sby/stg
obliged to sby/stg
pleased about/with sby/stg
ready for sby/stg
right about sby/stg
sad about sby/stg
satisfied with sby/stg
separate from stg
slow at (doing) stg
sorry about/for (doing) stg
surprised about/at/by
thankful to sby for stg
worried about sby/stg
wrong about sby/stg

Reporting verbs
(that) = can be omitted
accept that
agree (that); if/whether
answer that
ask somebody if/whether
assume (that)
believe (that)
bet (that)
certify that
claim (that)
complain (that)
conclude (that)
decide (that); if/whether
declare (that)
deny (that)
disagree that
doubt (that); if/whether
expect (that)
explain (that); whether
fancy (that)
fear (that)
feel (that)
find out (that); if/whether
gather (that); if/whether
guess (that); if/whether
(it) happens (that)
hope (that)
imagine (that)
imply (that)
indicate that
know (that); if/whether
learn (that); if/whether
mean (that)
note that
notice (that); if/whether
point out (that)
predict that
pretend (that)
promise (sby) (that)
prove (that); whether
realize (that)
record that
regret (that)
remark (= say) that
reply that
say (that); if/whether
state that
suggest (that)
suppose (that)
tell (me) (that); if/whether

Verb + *to***-infinitive**
(sby/stg) = optional object
allow sby
appoint sby
assist sby
attempt
begin
bribe sby
bring in sby
bring up sby
can't bear
cease
commence
condemn sby
consent
continue
dare
dare sby (= challenge)
deserve
elect sby
employ sby
enable sby
encourage sby
fail
get (sby/stg)
grow
hate sby
have (got)
hurry
like (sby/stg)
long
love (sby)
manage
need (sby/stg)
neglect
offer
pay (sby)
prefer (sby/stg)
refuse
rely on sby/stg
seek
select sby/stg
send (for) sby/stg
start
struggle
train (sby)
try
unite
(can't) wait
want (sby/stg)
wish (sby/stg)

APPENDIX 29 [> 16.4]
Verbs with and without objects
29.1 Some verbs which never take an object
My head **aches**.
ache, appear, arrive, come, cough, disappear, fall, go, sleep, sneeze.

29.2 Some verbs which may or may not take an object
I **opened the door**.
The door **opened**.
answer, ask, break, burn, close, drop, fly, grow, hurt, move, open, pull, ring, shake, shut, understand.

29.3 Some verbs which always take an object
We **enjoyed the play**.
afford, allow, blame, bring, contain, deny, enjoy, excuse, fetch, fix, get, have, let, like, love, make, need, prove, put.

APPENDIX 30 [> 16.7.3]
Conjunctions
30.1 Time
Clauses answer the question *When?*
I had a headache **when I got up this morning**.
after, as, as long as, as soon as, before, by the time (that), directly, during the time (that), immediately, the moment (that), now (that) once, since, until/till, when, whenever, while.

30.2 Place
Clauses answer the question *Where?*
She returned to the place **where she was born**.
anywhere, everywhere, where, wherever.

30.3 Manner
Clauses answer *How?*
He looks **as if he's seen a ghost**.
as if, as though, (in) the way, (in) the way that, (in) the same way, (in) the same way as.

30.4 Reason
Clauses answer the question *Why?*
We want a meal **because we're hungry**.
as, because, seeing (that), since.

30.5 Concession
Clauses introduce a contrast.
Though she's rich, *she lives quite simply*.
although, considering (that), though, even though, even if, much as ..., while, whereas, however much/badly/good, etc., no matter how, etc., *no matter how much*, etc.

30.6 Purpose
Clauses answer the question *What for?*
We arrived early **so that we could get tickets**.
so that, in order that, in case, lest, for fear that.

30.7 Result
Clauses describe consequences.
He's **so annoyed (that) you can't speak to him**.
so + adjective/adverb + *that*.

30.8 Comparison
Clauses introduce comparisons.
They answer *How ... compared with ...?*
I think she's more confident **than her brother is**.
as + adjective + *as* (as quick as), as + adverb + *as* (as quickly as), not so/as ... as, -er than, more ... than, less ... than, the ... the ... .

Points of time

yesterday	*today*	*tomorrow*
yesterday morning	*this morning*	*tomorrow morning*
yesterday at noon	*at noon*	*tomorrow at noon*
yesterday afternoon	*this afternoon*	*tomorrow afternoon*
yesterday evening	*this evening*	*tomorrow evening*
last night	*tonight*	*tomorrow night*

the day before yesterday
the night before last
the day before yesterday in
  the morning/afternoon

the day after tomorrow
the night after next
the day after tomorrow in
  the morning/afternoon

last Monday	*this Monday*	*next Monday*
the Monday before last		*the Monday after next*
last January	*this January*	*next January*
the January before last		*the January after next*
last Christmas	*this Christmas*	*next Christmas*
the Christmas before last		*the Christmas after next*
last week	*this week*	*next week*
the week before last		*the week after next*
last month	*this month*	*next month*
the month before last		*the month after next*
last year	*this year*	*next year*
the year before last		*the year after next*
last century	*this century*	*next century*
the century before last		*the century after next*

this time next week/next year, etc.
this time last week/last year, etc.

today week = a week from today
Tuesday week = a week from Tuesday
a week (or a fortnight, two weeks, a month) tomorrow
= a week, etc. *from tomorrow*

a week (or a fortnight, two weeks, a month) yesterday
= a week, etc. *from yesterday*

a week/two weeks/a fortnight from yesterday, from today/tomorrow
a month/two months from today, from tomorrow, from Monday, etc.
a month/two months last Tuesday, etc.
a month/two months next Tuesday, etc.

Index